Date Due

THE POWER OF MONEY

Also by Armand Van Dormael

BRETTON WOODS: Birth of a Monetary System

The Power of Money

Armand Van Dormael

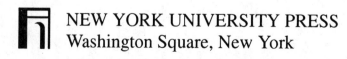

NEW YORK UNIVERSITY PRESS
Washington Square, New York

First published in the U.S.A. in 1997 by
NEW YORK UNIVERSITY PRESS
Washington Square
New York, N.Y. 10003

Library of Congress Cataloging-in-Publication Data
Van Dormael, Armand, 1916–
The power of money / Armand Van Dormael.
p. cm.
Includes bibliographical references and index.
ISBN 0–8147–8791–6
1. Money—Europe—History—20th century.   2. Money—United States–
–History—20th century.   3. Economic history—20th century.
I. Title.
HG220.E5V36   1997
332.4'9—dc20   96–35577
                                                                         CIP

Printed in Great Britain

For

Monique   Pierre   Jacques

Contents

1 The Power of Money

The world is awash with money. Every working day of the year $1 trillion
are exchanged between dealing rooms spread all over the planet and
linked by globe-spanning circuitry of satellites and fibre-optic cable.
Around the clock, electronic impulses project in a wink millions of
coded financial data on Reuter screens manned by dealers buying and
selling currencies, equities, futures, swaps, options, options on options
and even swaptions, either as a financial service to customers or in pro-
prietary trading. All the participants – they call themselves 'players' –
mostly large banks, claim their expertise is based on up-to-the-minute
global information and their advice on facts, not guesswork.

World population being 5.6 billion, the daily market turnover repre-
sents about $180 for every man, woman and child. International trade
amounts to $4 trillion a year. No computer is needed to figure that only
about 1 per cent of the foreign–exchange dealings is related to international business transactions. The rest is pure trading, serving no other
purpose than the management of investments or the assuagement of
the gambling instinct. Both are often intertwined in unavowable promis-
cuity.

Judging from the amount of liquid assets accumulated over the past
25 years, it is easier to get rich quick playing games with currencies than
producing goods. From Singapore to Capetown, from London to Los
Angeles, the international currency market keeps tens of thousands of
foreign-exchange dealers riveted all day long to their screens and telephones, in a hypermarket that knows no borders, only time zones. In this
singular global exchange, currencies and equities have become the most
widely traded commodities. Within less than three decades, a number of
groundbreaking innovations in financial engineering have broken down
national barriers, linked market to market through cross-border tax-
dodging money flows, matching capital and corporations, investors and
borrowers around the world. Bank branches, like so many tax-free
money shops, are ready to accommodate modest savers as well as institutional investors. According to the Bank for International Settlements,
borrowing on foreign markets rose from $36.4 billion in 1974 to $1.8 tril-
lion in 1993. From the very beginning, governments have been among the
most active borrowers.

Learned textbooks have always defined money as a unit of account, a
medium of exchange and a store of value, not as a commodity to be

1

traded like crude oil or soy beans. Recurrently, over the centuries, men have sought to master the secret of unlimited accretion of money. Gold, silver and copper had to be mined, refined and minted. The London goldsmiths of the seventeenth century were the first to discover with discreet amazement that they could write receipts – accepted as money – far in excess of the gold and silverware they held in safekeeping. Some became rich very quickly. But the temptation to overextend oneself was too great, inevitably leading to rumours which led to 'runs' by anxious depositors, often winding up in bankruptcy.

Only in the 1960s did London brokers 'invent' interbank lending, which finally allowed the international banking community to perform daily on a global scale the miracle of the loaves and the fishes. This money was not intended for commerce and industry but for speculation. From then on monetary liquidity has exponentially outrun the availability of tradeable goods and services as well as trustworthy borrowers. In commerce and industry, before anything can be distributed it must first be produced. In finance – and this may come as a shock to the uninitiated and even to some initiated – money is created out of thin air. Money in itself is not capital; to become capital it must be put to productive use.

Global foreign-exchange dealing is a recent phenomenon; throughout the ages the margin of profit on currency speculation was narrow and activities were confined to a few professionals. How did this new market develop and what do the liquid resources being shifted from one centre to another represent? This brings us to the fundamental question of the uses of money. 'Money', said Keynes, 'is only important for what it will procure.'

Money, properly used, has contributed immensely to humanity's economic development and material progress. Mismanagement and the abuse of money by those very people entrusted by society to be its guardians, have constituted a major cause of mankind's most crushing tragedies.

In monetary affairs, as in everything else, happy nations have no history. In our time certain dates and events stand out, where quarrels over money or frantic and irresponsible speculation played a major role. The Treaty of Versailles and the crash of 1929 were accidents of history setting off chain reactions culminating in World War II. Much of the human suffering they inflicted was the consequence of the inept or inexpert decisions by statesmen put at the helm of their governments by popular vote and the tumult of politics, but ungrounded in basic economics and unable to grasp the interrelated consequences of their policies.

Great leaders, political giants, blinded by hatred and primitive emotions, devoid of elementary economic common sense, applied political judgment to financial problems. Throughout the ages money was the hidden mainspring of major turning points in history, often underrated in the chronicles.

A banker such as Jakob Fugger has changed for ever the course of history in more ways than one. In 1519 he decided, after some hesitation, which of the two contenders would wear the crown of the Holy Roman Empire, Charles V, King of Spain or François I, King of France. The choice was the appanage of seven Electors. Both monarchs knew that the Electors' votes would cost a great deal of money. François I was the wealthiest. His bankers toured the Electors' residences with coffers full of gold écus, which they distributed generously in exchange for the solemn pledge that the vote would go to the King of France. Fugger sent out his emissaries with letters of credit payable *after* Charles V's election. He obviously won. This banking transaction may be considered the first major victory in history of credit over cash.

Reformation was largely born out of Luther's abhorrence of moneyed indulgences; he vituperated against the Fugger bank's practice of sending out a cashier to accompany each monk and pick up the money collected at the sermons. Fugger had indeed loaned a large sum to a young nobleman who wanted to buy three bishoprics; as a banker, he had the legitimate right to recuperate his funds. The pecuniary abuse of indulgences became the signal for the Protestant secession. It is doubtful whether any of the scores of men who fought and lost their lives on the battlefields, in defence of their faith, had any notion of their rulers' motives in the decision to side with the Catholics or the Protestants.

The horrors of Nazism have obliterated from the collective memory and from world conscience the fact that Hitler owed his rise to power mainly to a twofold breakdown of the German money system; after the trauma of trillions of worthless paper marks came a depression leaving millions of unemployed without any cash to buy food. The devastating sufferings inflicted upon the German people by the 1923 hyperinflation followed by the sudden deflation of 1930 destroyed the wealth and the values of the most solid elements in society, leaving behind a moral and economic vacuum, breeding ground for the disasters which followed. Millions of destitute men and women put their hope in a leader who promised them dignity, work and bread. Hitler's *Putsch* took place 12 days before the stabilization of the German mark. In 1924 the National Socialist party won 32 seats in the Reichstag. In 1929, after a few years of growing prosperity, they were reduced to 12. Hitler's party had become totally marginal, almost non-existent. In 1930, after the reverberations of the Wall Street crash threw an uncomprehending German nation into despair for the second time in a decade, through no fault of its own, 107 Nazis won seats in the Reichstag; in July 1932 there were 230. From then on, the wrecking of Germany's financial structure, inflicted largely from outside, endangered the economic order and the political security of Europe. The life of nations is a matrix in which cause becomes result and result cause.

When history records conflicts between nations and communities divided by deep-rooted ideals and convictions, or the deadly con frontation of millions of people engaged in a total war, the primary role of money in the genesis of these antagonisms often becomes blurred and overwhelmed by indispensable propaganda and the thunder of arms.

In the seamless and tumultuous web of recent history a few dates and events stand out as turning points in the course of mankind's fate. Money was at the centre of the Treaty of Versailles, the crash of 1929, the Bretton Woods Agreements and their demise.

The state of an economy depends mainly on the material and cultural legacy of bygone generations, upon which the personal abilities and entrepreneurial initiative, the diligence of employers and employees can build additional prosperity.

Commerce and industry are by far the most efficacious segments of any modern society and constitute the indispensable backbone of the economy. Sustained economic growth also depends to a large extent upon the smooth working of a banking and credit system. Governments can influence a market economy – for better or for worse – through a limited number of economic instruments at their disposal: interest rates, taxation, spending. Despite common guise and pretence, they cannot control it, but they can signpost.

The national and international bureaucracies they engender, while providing secure employment, invariably tend to become bloated, self-sufficient and self-perpetuating bodies with questionable useful potential. For example, of the statutory function of the International Monetary Fund (IMF) as guardian of exchange rates and regulator of international liquidity, only the trappings and the decorum remain, which gives the institution an air of unreality, not to say surreality.

Europe has recovered remarkably from the calamities of war and rebuilt its house, not as a cluster of separate introverted entities but as a group of nations working their way toward some form of union.

For more than two decades after World War II, under the rules of Bretton Woods, Europe experienced its most remarkable surge in living standards ever. Prosperity came to be taken for granted as the natural order of things. It generated problems of overemployment. Several governments chose to resort to massive immigration of foreign workers from Turkey, North Africa and elsewhere, without giving the slightest thought to the second, third and following generations.

As long as it functioned smoothly, hardly anybody was aware of the existence of a monetary system. International trade was carried out on a secure basis. Only when repeated attacks by currency speculators brought the system down and monetary crises became the recurrent pabulum of the daily press, did the people involved in international trade become conscious of the importance and value of a stable currency system.

Each crisis went through a similar ritual: bouts of speculation against one or several currencies, European finance ministers expressing confidence in the stability of the system, triggering off redoubled speculative attacks, countered by clumsy central bank intervention; inevitably there followed the perplexed and disgruntled statements by finance ministers peevishly admitting defeat or glossing over the incident with cosmetic phrases. The speculators, alive to the value of silence in a battle of wits, were never heard nor seen, but on each occasion their public relations arm, the British and American financial press, triumphantly and jokingly poked fun at 'those silly ministers' who should have left financial affairs to the bankers.

In the process, the international banking community gradually eroded national sovereignties, becoming an unseen power within the state and wielding considerable influence over public affairs. The European governments were thus forced to share with the international banking community their most prized national prerogatives of sovereignty: the parity of their currencies and their monetary policy.

Contrary to general beliefs, there is nothing mysterious about the causes, the mechanism and the interests at stake in monetary crises. The collapse of the Bretton Woods system in the early 1970s was followed by a boom. Soon the delicate mechanism balancing production, consumption, investment and employment was stalled, causing the worst recession since the Great Depression. Ever since, unemployment has been Europe's major plague. Outside the field of oratory, not much has come out of government offices indicating possible relief.

Although living standards remain extremely high, for the first time in recent history a generation of youngsters has every reason to believe that they will be less secure and prosperous than their parents.

We have not yet learned to cope with the problems of unemployment or overemployment. The consequences of unemployment are immediately visible; a time lag hangs over the long-term observable sequels of overemployment. Nobody can foretell or even evaluate what the presence of millions of undereducated, often unschooled but prolific, Islamic and largely ghettoed people in the run-down quarters of our European cities holds in store.

Moreover, the question may be asked whether waxing affluence as a result of an accelerating wage upswing, another by-product of overemployment, will content the populace. Whatever the level of welfare, conflicts over the sharing of its bounty are bound to continue. The great student revolt of May 1968 was sparked by well-off young people, coming predominantly from middle-class families, who rebelled against what they saw as a money-ridden and hidebound society, at a moment when prosperity had reached its all-time peak in France.

This book has been a long time in the making. Opinions and theories are easy to come by. Research in international monetary affairs is hurdled with ambushes saturated with questionable authoritative assertions and opaque commentary.

It takes time to separate veracity from verisimilitude, but once this has been achieved, it becomes possible to look backwards with extraordinary clarity. Retrothinking is obviously easier than forward planning. Analysis of the past, however, is important because of the light it sheds on the prospects for the future.

The task of the researcher is to understand and explain, without weeding or sifting, while trying to go to the core of the matter.

This is a detached analysis of facts, researched and recorded without postulates, without any tampering or reservations, intended to fill a void. The independent and empirical investigator, uninhibited by national or corporate parameters, not accountable to any organization or establishment, does not have to shove anything under the rug and can exert the gratifying freedom of letting the chips fall where they may.

No offence is intended and no controversy sought. The facts, as they are related, do not call for much comment nor any appraisal. No stone is cast. By what criteria could one be guided anyway when sitting in judgment over power games about the control of money?

From time immemorial, ideas and principles about money have slowly evolved in the laboratory of history under the tests and pressures of practical experience and the dynamics of change. Until very recently, evolution was slow and guarded: coins still have the same appearance and function as the Greek coins minted 2400 years ago, except they do not exude the same breathtaking beauty. A banknote is still a rectangular piece of paper bearing a signature; it is very similar in appearance and identical in function to the seventeenth-century banknotes of the London goldsmith-bankers.

Throughout the centuries money has been a jealously guarded national prerogative: only the monarch, the political authority, and later the central bank, had power over the nation's currency. An international medium of exchange was unthinkable.

This book describes how, through an improbable chain of events, a few million Chinese-owned dollars-in-hiding developed during the Korean war into a secret parallel market before coming out into the open, and finally ruled the world's finances, sweeping aside government-elaborated systems such as Bretton Woods and the European Monetary System (EMS).

No guidebook is available to steer the puzzled but inquisitive searcher for truth through the mass of scholarly works and the multitude of tendentious but superficially plausible writings published under the cloak of objective analysis. 'The study of money, above all other fields in economics,' says Professor Galbraith, 'is one in which complexity is used to disguise truth or to evade truth, not to reveal it.'[1] Milton Friedman, who disagrees with Galbraith about everything else, concurs: 'In monetary matters, appearances are deceiving; the important relationships are often precisely the reverse of those that strike the eye.'[2]

This book is an attempt to set the record straight. The reader unversed in economic jargon or theory should not be deterred by the prospect of having to explore scientific arcana. Scholarship in economics is of marginal use in international monetary affairs and will hardly be mentioned; when it is resorted to by self-seeking politicians around the negotiating table, promulgated and bent to the needs of the day by eminent economists or propagated by flag-waving commentators, it is generally no more than a cog used to underprop an argument intended to protect a corporate interest or justify a national policy.

Ever since August 1993 European currencies have been floating. Relative calm prevails over the exchange markets, disturbed occasionally by bouts of speculation: a simple reminder by the currency traders that they are in control.

The outcome of the battles waged and directed from the board-rooms in the Manhattan skyscrapers against the seemingly im-pregnable European central-bank fortresses, between those responsible to the people for 'the common good' and those responsible to their shareholders for 'profit maximization' was foreseeable and a foregone conclusion.

Over the past century a group of banking dynasties has built an unseen, unstructured but closely interconnected financial empire with the proven power to unmake any government-elaborated monetary system.

This book relates the conflict between sovereign states and stateless economic forces, the struggle for supremacy between the political authorities and the financial community, their alternate victories and setbacks, their tactics and strategies, their strengths and weaknesses.

The advent of international currencies has given rise to a new breed of adventurous financiers, reminiscent of the frontier, very different in out-look and demeanour from the traditional conservative banker. The nat-ure of their business has radically changed: from lenders they have become traders. The princes of finance and the bankers of bygone centu-ries, the Fuggers, John Law, the Barings, the Rothschilds, Bleichröder and the generations of Jewish moneylenders who once manipulated coins and receipts when the Church condemned usury as a mortal sin, never tried to supplant the rulers they served. They gave additional power to the powerful, endowing ambitious men with the means to fulfil their aspirations, while making sure they would be repaid on time. This forced them, above anyone else, to peer into the future, and to anticipate conditions at the time their money was due. They did not speculate: they reasoned and prefigured. While pulling the strings of power, they did not exert power. Almost all were very wealthy. Not all were very moral.

The first banker openly and successfully to challenge political power was John Pierpont Morgan. Against the will of successive presidents and governments, he dominated and organized American finances and industry as he saw fit, building the most gigantic financial and industrial empire the world had seen. Breaking with tradition, he established the primacy of finance over industry. Nearly all of the largest American cor-porations were closely linked through stock ownership and interlocking directorships, which he controlled. His spiritual heirs, the executives of Morgan's banks, their affiliates and allies have continued for over a cen-tury to expand the empire. They exert today unquestioned leadership over the financial markets. They made many costly mistakes, bringing some of their own corporations to the brink of the precipice; but in their

contest with European governments over the control of the world's foreign-exchange markets, they won all the battles. During the current waiting game, which started in August 1993, they will cash in the huge benefits of floating rates, poised for the next round.

That is the way it is. History goes its unpredictable and unstoppable route. Once more we are drifting in uncharted waters, with unreliable compasses and instruments as our main recourse, probing the present, mapping out the future.

2 The Morganization of America

There's the place and here's the pen.

John Pierpont Morgan

Of all the bankers who once manipulated huge amounts of money and inflected the course of history, only John Pierpont Morgan still casts his shadow over world finance. Long before his death in Rome in 1913 he had become the recognized 'Caesar of Wall Street'. Yet, by Wall Street standards, his declared fortune was not exceedingly large; several of his partners and a number of business magnates owned much more money than he.

John Pierpont Morgan wanted power. He considered himself and was looked upon as the most powerful man in the United States and nobody dared challenge him except, occasionally, President Theodore Roosevelt. Friend and foe regarded him as their superior. The financial empire he built, highly interlocked but unstructured, institutionalized and, for over a century, constantly aggrandized by his spiritual heirs, the managers of the banks he founded or controlled, is today more powerful and cohesive than ever.

Just as J. P. Morgan's stewardship once ruled the finances and much of the economy of the United States, openly challenging the antitrust laws and the President's authority to intervene in the organization and the planning of the economy, his successors, in control of the global currency market have challenged and breached the government's sovereign prerogative to set the exchange rates and determine monetary policy. Although this challenge is never publicly expressed through statements or communiqués by the banking community, the facts are there for everyone to see: the Eurodollar dominates world finance. The currencies of the major trading nations float, their value being set by the mood of the market. The once-powerful finance ministers and central bankers are constantly reminded that the market may undo much of what they decide and that, before making any decision, they must always consider how the market will react.

JOHN PIERPONT MORGAN

John Pierpont Morgan's personality, the rock upon which he built his empire, is unique in financial history. The Rothschilds, the Fuggers, the Medici and the Barings acquired wealth and authority mostly through cunning and resourcefulness. Morgan was possessed by the urge to dominate and command; he displayed the right combination of vision and organizing ability.

His father, J. Spencer Morgan, was a very successful American banker established in London. In 1868 he set up a branch in Paris. Much of the British investments in American railroads and industry were cleared through his company. His most celebrated coup was the organization of a syndicate which floated $50 million in French government bonds in 1870, when Prussian troops were still besieging Paris. The syndicate took a 10 per cent commission and the loan enabled France to advance the payment of the indemnity demanded by Bismarck and thus shorten the occupation of the country. The London-based Morgan bank became a legend, co-equal with the Rothschilds and the Barings.

Young John Pierpont travelled throughout Europe and went to school in Switzerland. He spent two years at the University of Göttingen. To the castle born, abrupt and domineering, he aggressively displayed an inbred arrogance of caste. He established himself as a banker near Wall Street, specializing in foreign exchange. When the Civil War broke out, like every armed conflict, 'a rich man's war and a poor man's fight', he paid a stand-in to replace him in the army. He also financed some dubious but very lucrative arms sales to the government. He was implicated in a 'scandal' involving gold speculation, but was never indicted.

Cosmopolitan in education and outlook, he stood head and shoulders above his peers. He had an intuitive grasp of any given situation and the ability to decide instantly what he wanted. Accountable only to himself, he always took full responsibility for his decisions.

The country was young. Transforming what was still partly a wilderness into a complex industrial nation required almost unlimited quantities of capital. This was the age of the robber barons and of generalized skullduggery: an amalgam of ruthless speculation, savage competition, political and business corruption. Buccaneers swooped upon and seized railroads largely built with public money on public land. The railroads were free from government control on the theory of private competitive enterprise. The government must pay but must not interfere. Corporate manipulation, intimidation, the crushing of competitors as well as stock jugglery were common practice. Money corrupted politicians, judges and newspapermen. Politics had become a business, the source of many a fortune.

Railroad companies signed agreements with important customers, discriminating against their competitors. John D. Rockefeller characterized the age in his systematic use of discriminatory railroad rates. He not only made it difficult for competitors to ship oil, every barrel they did ship yielded him a profit.

Within a few years the new Morgan bank became the most important institution in New York engaged in international finance, providing British investment capital to American industry, an activity comparatively neglected by other American banking houses. But Morgan's domineering and truculent character, animated by an overwhelming urge to establish his power, could not be satisfied with the restricted function of the investment banker as an intermediary between the corporate enterprise and the investor. The traditional function of the banks had been the financing of industry and of the mercantile movement of its products. The merchant capitalist was the dominant entrepreneurial factor.

In 1869, aged 32, Morgan engaged in a struggle with two promoters who were plundering the Erie railroad. He met them on their own terms, force against force, trick against trick, and beat them. Ten years later he controlled 30 railroad companies; he had definitely emerged as the dominant power in American finance, an organizing genius with well-established operations and unique affiliations in Europe.

The *New York Times* described a conference attended by several railroad presidents as a banker's triumph and a president's surrender. The paper coined a new word: 'Morganization'. It meant the control of finance over industry and the centralization of industry and finance. A trust was Morgan's notion of the ideal way to organize industry.

By inclination he was a conservative banker, of impeccable integrity with his partners and associates. In addition to his banking activities he participated directly in a variety of corporate affairs, combining, consolidating, centralizing and imposing the mastery of finance over industry through the institutionalized control of investment resources gathered by the sale of securities to innumerable American and foreign investors, mainly British and German. In the process he put an end to the unrestrained and ruthless competition which had prevailed and which he considered inefficient, wasteful and destructive.

Morgan personified the revolution which transformed the financier from an agent of industry to its master. The interlocking of finance and industry constitutes the first and fundamental characteristic of the process of Morganization.

A book published in 1930, *The House of Morgan*, describes the uniqueness of the bank as follows:

> At every important stage in the development of the House of Morgan there is the shaping influence of international finance. They are almost inseparable. Activity in international finance first helped the Morgans secure American financial power and then the world financial power they now possess. The earlier stage expressed the immaturity of American capitalism, the later its maturity, while the whole period expresses the development of world capitalism and of financial imperialism. There is a complex interplay of national and international forces, the dynamic movement of which decisively influenced the rise to power of the House of Morgan.[1]

The process of financial centralization and control expressed itself in the domination of the House, but equally through the personal ascendancy and dictatorship of Morgan himself. His overwhelming impulse to dominate, to rule and to have this rulership accepted, was the decisive factor in his rise to eminence and in the supremacy of his bank.

Bankers, by the very nature of their institutional function, normally appear in an enterprise after it is established and successful. Finance is regulative, not creative. With Morgan, money became the supreme power, determining production and consumption. Morganization thus usurped financial control of industry. Inevitably his will to establish monopolies would clash with the government and public opinion animated by the ideal of free competition between a large number of enterprises. He became the symbol of 'money power'.

Small businessmen were crushed by ever-growing trusts. Farmers raised crops but the railroads made more money in one day by carrying the crops to the cities than farmers made in a season. Monopoly and combination were against the interests of the people. Populist leaders vowed to break up the industrial complexes which dominated both worker and farmer. Among factory workers the labour movement was on the rise; populist and anti-capitalist sentiment was widespread. The concentration of wealth by a few industrial and financial magnates, contemptuous of the public and arrogant toward labour, caused strong resentment. Pioneers settled in the wilderness upon the promise of a railroad which never came, and had to abandon their land. Elected state legislators opposed to 'money power' tried to regulate railroads but their legislation was nullified by court decisions.

In 1893 Morgan enhanced his authority by coming to the rescue of a troubled government. A depression hit the country and European investors started selling their American securities, forcing the Treasury to export its gold. The outflow, added to the deficiency of government resources, produced a panic: banks and the public hoarded gold and the Treasury's reserve fell below the statutory limit. There loomed the danger that specie payments would have to be suspended. The Treasury tried to secure gold by a public issue of bonds. The bids were so slow that failure appeared probable. Helpless in the emergency, unable to solve the problem, the government reluctantly turned to Morgan who stopped the crisis, but on his own 'extremely harsh' terms. Measuring with little mercy the distress of the government, he enjoyed the privilege of being able to drive a hard bargain with Washington.

President Theodore Roosevelt represented the 'little man', the farmer, the worker. Privately he courted big business but publicly he railed against cartels and trusts and pilloried the 'malefactors of great wealth'. His campaign for the regulation of trusts and railroads caused several clashes with Morgan. Rockefeller's oil companies were found guilty of violating the Anti-Trust Act and forced to pay heavy fines.

Roosevelt had vowed to punish 'successful dishonesty'. The magnates, accustomed to buying political subservience with campaign contributions, resented Roosevelt's accepting their money and then denouncing them. They were not used to 'getting nothing for their money'.

Morgan's temperamental dislike of Roosevelt ultimately developed into violent, unreasoning hatred, which fed on itself and on events.

> Morgan looked upon Roosevelt as a sometimes irresponsible child-man who could usually be trusted to act 'correctly' in most situations. He realized that the antitrust campaign was more bombast and spectacular by-play than an actual attempt to revamp the structure of American business. Nonetheless, at times Teddy could get quite stubborn, and then no one on earth could make him change his mind. For years the Administration had seemed uneasy about the huge U.S. Steel complex, Morgan's major claim to fame and one of his proudest creations.[2]

Now Morgan wanted to buy an additional steel company but the acquisition was blocked by price considerations and Administration policies. The year was 1907 and the Knickerbocker Trust panic, one of the most severe ever, was shaking the nation. Morgan was the only man who could stop it if he wanted. This was an occasion, he thought, to force the President to let him go ahead. He sent the two top men of US Steel to

Roosevelt. They told the President that if he did not authorize the merger, the investment banking house that controlled the steel company might collapse and usher in an even worse panic that would disrupt the economy for a long time to come. Roosevelt had no choice but to accept the merger; the President of the United States capitulated to J. P. Morgan. During and after the 1907 panic it was frequently charged that dominant financial interests, particularly the House of Morgan and its affiliates, had deliberately engineered the crisis in order to crush competitors and magnify their own power by larger centralization and control.[3]

Morgan paid his new acquisition in US Steel shares, not in cash. It later appeared that the property, when developed, would be worth ten times the price he paid. US Steel, producing two-thirds of the national output, the greatest combination of mergers the world had ever seen and which he organized with Rockefeller's help, was his greatest triumph.

Convinced that governments should not get involved in industry and finance which they do not understand and where they do more harm than good, he relentlessly fought off every attempt to probe his operations. What was competition and what was monopoly? How big was 'big' when it came to the steel industry?

Emerging triumphant out of the panic, Morgan consolidated his empire. His Bankers Trust Co. absorbed the Trust Company of America; shortly after, with his partners, he bought a substantial share of Guaranty along with Mutual Life's holdings. Tightening his control of New York Life, he bought control of Equitable Life, becoming dominant in the three largest insurance companies of the country.

At the end of his life there was no one to dispute J. P. Morgan's supremacy in the system of financial control and centralization over which he towered, unchallenged in its mastery. Over his competitors he had the advantage of being a financier and finance was the power centre of the system. He was not the most brilliant financier, but he was a ruler capable of imposing himself through personal authority where the others depended largely on institutional authority. Wall Street trusted Morgan because he was dependable, a necessary quality of sustained dictatorship.

John Pierpont Morgan died in 1913. He had entertained the Kaiser on his yacht, he had met with popes, kings and dignitaries. A great womanizer and a great moralizer, a prominent Episcopal layman, he had travelled throughout Europe amassing a formidable art collection.

During his lifetime he *was* the Morgan bank. By means of voting trusts, stock ownership and directorships J. P. Morgan & Co. controlled or dominated First National Bank, National City Bank, three trust companies and three life insurance companies. By the same means he dominated ten great railroad systems, and five of the largest industrial corporations: US Steel, General Electric, American Telephone & Telegraph, International Harvester and Western Union.

The Morgan partners held 72 interlocking directorships in 47 of the largest corporations with more than $10 billion in resources or capitalization. The House of Morgan, moreover, completely dominated Bankers Trust, Guaranty Trust and National Bank of Commerce whose officers and directors held upward of 300 interlocking directorships, many of them in corporations not under immediate control or influence of the bank.[4]

Responsible only to himself and to his close associates and partners, he was the complete reactionary with an outspoken contempt of politicians, which he considered an inferior breed. Like most members of his class he accepted politics as the protector of privileges and spoils, but was aghast at politics being used to promote larger social interests. The Federal taxation of corporate and personal incomes was condemned by the magnates as 'confiscatory' and as the precursor of socialism. According to one banker: 'The Government, instead of taxing incomes, ought to pay premium to men achieving financial success.' Tax avoidance is a right and, since it increases profits, almost a moral obligation.

John Pierpont Morgan Jr dynastically succeeded his father; the founder's death produced no effect on the system of centralization. It had become institutionalized and accepted by the industrial and financial community; it cast off personal dictatorship, functioning instead in terms of the dictatorship of an institutional self-perpetuating and self-regulating oligarchy. Its financial resources gradually expanded to exceed by far anything the elder Morgan had known. The system continued to function smoothly and nobody stepped forward to claim title to his succession. Times had changed and so had manners.

When World War I broke out the City expected for a while to be the banker of the allies. It soon became evident that the enormous quantities of American war material had to be paid for in gold and securities. About 70 per cent of American shares and bonds owned by British and French citizens, and accumulated over many decades, had to be sold. The war conferred political world power to the United States and in its wake financial world power to the House of Morgan.

In August 1914 the French government deposited six million dollars' worth of gold with the Paris branch of the Morgan bank to open a credit in New York for purchases in the United States. At the outbreak of the war the British government designated the Morgan bank as its commercial agent with exclusive control over all purchases in the United States. Most of these purchases were kept 'in the family'. In October 1915, when British resources became exhausted, Morgan arranged for a loan of $500 million to be spent by the allies on American purchases. The Morgan loans and purchases revived American industry and started an upward movement of prosperity. The war had become a war of munitions, of machinery and Morgan was on the side of the allies.

When it became known that a syndicate of American bankers came to the help of Britain and France, the press greeted the event with hyperbole: 'Uncle Sam, Banker of the World', 'Europe Bankrupt', 'The Dollar becomes World Currency' shouted the headlines. Wall Street bankers seriously began to have ambitions to make New York the financial centre of the world.

For years the Populist party accused the government of having entered a war which did not concern the United States, mainly to protect Morgan's financial interests. After the war American financial supremacy became obvious during the numerous conferences held to untangle the snarl created by the reparations imbroglio. When it became evident that the governments would be unable to solve the problem, J. P. Morgan Jr proposed to let his bank take the matter out of politics and put it on a commercial basis. He organized the syndicate which floated billions of dollars of German bonds on the American market: as it turned out, the banks made a lot of money, Germany used the dollars to pay its reparations debt to the allies and the unwary American investors wound up owning worthless bonds.

In 1926 the bank granted a loan to the French government embroiled in a monetary crisis: the same year Mussolini's Italy and many other countries also resorted to the Morgan bank for financial assistance to help them stabilize their currencies. The international prestige of the Morgan name had never been higher.

Dominant in foreign loans, the Morgan bank and its affiliates also financed the foreign investment of American companies. Radio Corporation of America, a Morgan affiliate, was interlocked with General Electric, ITT, Westinghouse; General Motors; ATT, United Fruit and so on. ITT controlled telephones, cables, telegraphs, radio and electrical manufacturing in 30 countries. All these companies were bound together through interlocking directorates with each other and with the Morgan bank.

Guaranty Trust, First National and Bankers Trust were Morgan affiliates while National City and Chase National Bank were allies. Together they controlled one-third of American banking resources and two-thirds of the country's insurance assets.[5]

In 1929 J. P. Morgan Jr and his 17 partners held 99 directorships in 72 industrial, financial and railroad corporations and utilities, all among the largest in America.

The Morgan bank did not control these corporations or the system itself. It simply acted as the balance wheel to maintain cohesion. There were wheels within wheels, competing financial groups, some of which were as large as the Morgan bank. There was also considerable rivalry. 'In sum, financial centralization and control comprise an industrial and financial government largely sufficient unto itself and responsible primarily to its oligarchical manipulators.'[6]

Morganization, the centralization of industry and finance, imposing financial control over industry, introduced coordination and regulation, the goal being the coordination and regulation of profits. In 1904 John Moody concluded that the Rockefeller and Morgan groups could not be considered as separate financial entities, so intertwined were their interlocking directorships and stock ownerships.

> Taking another look at the Rockefeller–Morgan empire in the mid-1960s, Peter Dooley concludes that 'it is not possible to separate these groups'. The power base of the Rockefeller–Morgan group is the control of six of the country's largest banks: the Chase Manhattan Bank, the Rockefeller family depository, of which David Rockefeller is chairman; the First National City Bank; Manufacturers Hanover Trust; the Chemical Bank of New York; the Morgan Guaranty Trust, and Bankers Trust.[7]

The same group, a collection of nominally separate corporations, united by a common interest through the pooling of their resources, thus enhancing their combined power, managed by the descendants, beneficiaries and employees of John D. Rockefeller and John Pierpont Morgan, today control the world's financial markets. They *are* the market-makers with tens of thousands of dealers spread all over the globe. They alone had the global power to decide when and where a currency or an international monetary system established by governments should be attacked. The financial gurus who occasionally parade before the press, bragging about their victories over central banks, are dwarfs or nonentities; but they serve a purpose as convenient scapegoats, 'gnomes' and smoke screens, targets ready to absorb the wrath of politicians against speculators during and after each monetary crisis. Only the Morgan–Rockefeller empire had the power to decide that Bretton Woods, which it furiously opposed, should be suppressed because there is little money to be made with fixed exchange rates staying within 1 per cent of parity. For the same reason, it decided to liquidate the European monetary system. It took three years to unmake Bretton Woods and only three days to dismantle the EMS.

Ever since Franklin Roosevelt disappeared from the scene, Wall Street has owned the United States Treasury lock, stock and barrel. Europe, a financial dependency of the empire, with its daydreaming about a monetary union, stood in its way. Although it happened before our eyes, very few in the European establishment realized who wrecked its Exchange Rate Mechanism (ERM). Today's financial dynasts do not stand for a family but for a corporation. The system dominates, institutionalized in the operations of the large banks, the dictatorship oligarchical, its manipulators being glorified clerks rather than the flaming buccaneers of the past.

Walter Wriston, for years chairman of Citibank, and the epitome of the Morgan–Rockefeller empire, was by far the most enterprising banker of our time. He embodies and perpetuates the Morgan spirit which, more than ever, permeates the international banking community, when he states that individual liberty 'requires constant defense against the encroachment of the State'.

> So far, however, world capital markets have managed systematically to adjust and preserve the world's economic balance without waiting for governments to tell them how to do it. In fact, the markets are usually well on their way to solving a problem about the time the regulators become aware of it and start gearing up to tell us how to manage it. When the first OPEC oil crisis occurred in 1973, there was immense anxiety over both a shortage of domestic oil and a surplus of money flowing to the Middle East oil-producing states. . . . The successful adjustments to the quadrupling of oil prices in 1973 and 1974 became one of the most dramatic episodes in economic history.[8]

Wriston took great pride in his role as originator of the recycling of petrodollars who put his stamp of leadership on the largest and fastest transfer of funds in history. Nobody else indeed stepped forward to solve the problem. So the banks enthusiastically lent enormous amounts of dollars to poor countries; much of the money was not invested as expected, but sent abroad or used to pay for imports. When it appeared that a number of countries would never repay their debts and would not even pay interest, the banks stopped lending. After years of wrangling, the IMF and the World Bank, prodded by the United States government, somehow disentangled the knot.

> Walter Wriston in New York ran a phantasmagorical bank in which profits were merely reported and never earned; the loans never were and never would be repaid, and the borrowers could not afford to carry them. Increasingly, the interest on these foreign loans, which Citicorp reported as revenue, was merely another loan from the bank to the borrower, building reported assets faster than reported liabilities, but yielding no cash flow.[9]

Shortly after Wriston's retirement his successor had to announce that $3 billion was being put in the bank's loan loss reserves for Latin America. It was the biggest single write-off ever. It meant a 'hit' to Citicorp's bottom line, ending the year with a loss unprecedented in American banking.[10] It had no bearing on the fortunes of the Morgan–Rockefeller empire.

3 Germany Will Pay

Paris, 18 January 1919: after more than four years of warfare an armistice had been signed. The Peace Conference was to begin. Millions of people who did not want to become heroes, had been marched to destruction by order of their warlords and by the dictates of international diplomacy.

Flushed with victory, breaking President Wilson's solemn pledge of a 'just and honorable' peace which had led the belligerents to sign the Armistice, the allies decided, in keeping with tradition, to make the vanquished pay. The hour of reckoning had come. Clemenceau's forceful personality dominated the deliberations. He was convinced that: 'Humanity's pertinacious problem, since it is permanently engaged in rival activities, is to always live in confrontation, only to get along temporarily. . . . The war, officially terminated, continues in a different form, called pacification.'[1]

At Versailles, six months later, the Peace Treaty was presented to the Germans as an ultimatum:

> The English and American negotiators said: 'Germany can only pay if its economy is restored. It should know the extent of its obligations. And obviously, the lower they are the easier will be the settlement.' We said: 'Germany must fully pay all the damage it has caused to people and property. If this principle is not recognized, there will be no just peace.' The French position prevailed. . . . Our triumph was short-lived.[2]

President Wilson had expressed stupefaction at the size of the bills presented by France and its allies. The Belgians demanded for their own share a sum larger than the entire wealth of the country and, since they had been invaded first, they wanted to be paid first, thus arousing Clemenceau's anger.

A few lucid men warned the statesmen and the public that a future European order based upon revenge and the exaction of an unbearable war booty would intolerably burden the children and grandchildren of the vanquished and perpetuate the hatreds the war had unleashed, with unforeseeable consequences.

No one was more outspoken than a young Englishman, John Maynard Keynes. An economist, he analysed Germany's potential to pay reparations and calculated that the amounts demanded would mortgage the future of two generations, taking away the fruits of their labour. Using a vast amount of facts and figures, he demonstrated that, economically, the demands were unrealistic. He was severely criticized as a 'defeatist' and his warnings were dismissed.

In *The Economic Consequences of the Peace*, a book that made him world-famous overnight, he castigated the ignorance, the intrigues and the state of mind of the men who had laid down the terms of the Treaty. Clemenceau, said Keynes, was an old man, living in the past, with a com pelling passion to undo 1870, to spoliate Germany and to keep France's inexorable, secular and mortal enemy prostrated as long as possible. It was utterly unrealistic to expect that the German people, amputated of their productive capacity, would be able and willing to pay in gold and merchandise the enormous amounts demanded. He warned:

> Economic privation proceeds by easy stages, and so long as men suffer it patiently, the outside world cares little. Physical efficiency and resistance to disease slowly diminish, but life proceeds somehow, until the limit of human endurance is reached at last and counsels of despair and madness stir the sufferers from the lethargy which precedes the crisis. Then man shakes himself, sovereign, and he listens to whatever instruction of hope, illusion or revenge is carried to him on the air.[3]

The Versailles Treaty has now receded into the realm of history as one of the greatest diplomatic mistakes and dramas of all times. Men's minds, warped by the ordeal of war, had been unable to see the future on any other basis than that a defeated nation should pay for its misdeeds. Instead of redeeming Europe, divided against itself, it perpetuated the sentiment of 'sacred patriotism' and exasperated hatreds and fears, provoking 20 years of economic warfare. It sowed the seeds of disintegration of the order it intended to establish.

Europe, still the nerve centre of the world, its empires covering the globe, lay exhausted while the United States reached the status of world power. Even before the negotiations were completed, President Wilson had returned home, unable to understand European intrigues, trickery and selfishness. The Senate refused to ratify the Treaty and the United States withdrew from the entanglements of the Old World, except that it demanded payment, to the last dollar, for all the supplies and war material the government and private citizens had sold on credit to the belligerents, mainly Britain and France. These had been commercial transactions to be honoured as any commercial transaction should be.

The war debts amounted to $10.3 billion and the allies were bankrupt. Much of their gold had crossed the Atlantic during the war to pay for American supplies. The amount of reparations was set at 132 billion gold marks to be converted into dollars or into the creditors' currencies. In addition, Germany had to abandon its colonies and a substantial part of its territory, deliver the vast majority of its merchant ships, its fishing fleet, 5000 locomotives, 150 000 railroad cars, 5000 trucks and all the material left behind in the combat zones. Furthermore, all foreign investments were apt to be confiscated. The reparations bill was justified by the war guilt clause, which made Germany solely responsible for the conflict.

The German people never accepted this historical analysis nor the moral assumption on which the whole idea of reparations was based. The controversy would, over the years, grow into a test of wills.

Gold marks did not exist any more; nor did the gold francs in which the French claims were made. At the outbreak of the war the European belligerents had suspended the conversion of their paper currencies into gold; gold coins had been withdrawn from circulation. The American dollar remained convertible.

The gold standard gone, the exchange rates of currencies were determined by the free play of supply and demand. The 'rules of the game', the automatic checks of the gold standard no longer existed and no new technique to replace them had been mastered nor even considered. The mode of thought of the men who dominated politics and finance was determined by a deep-rooted tradition based on their lifetime experience.

These men failed to notice that the old order had become obsolete. To them the gold standard was still the only basis upon which international financial relations could be built. It would inevitably be restored and currencies would be convertible again at their normal pre-war rate.

International monetary relations were not the domain of governments. It was expected that national and international finance, in the hands of central banks – private institutions – would continue to manage itself. No one seemed to realize that the gold standard had in fact been a sterling standard, a transitory mechanism based on the ability of the City to maintain a balance between assets and liabilities in world trade. This phase of British history had been closed by the war. The City's credit system was built upon confidence and its material basis was gold. When one goes the other fails.

THE GERMAN INFLATION OF 1923

The ink on the Treaty of Versailles was hardly dry when the allies started demanding payment of reparations. To satisfy the pressing demands of the victors the German government had to buy francs and other currencies with paper marks. Since Berlin had practically no exchange market, the Reichsbank appointed Fritz Mannheimer as its agent in Amsterdam. Shielded from the war, Amsterdam had become a very important financial centre.

A German citizen, Mannheimer had been an obscure broker in Paris before the war. He escaped conscription and had been sent to Holland at the beginning of the conflict as head of foreign procurement for the army. Several times he had become involved in fraudulent operations, but had been protected by Dutch politicians. A corpulent, full-blooded man of immense energy and imagination, he was again sent to Amsterdam, this time to procure foreign currency for the Reichsbank. Wilhelm Vocke, who was later to become the first president of the Bundesbank, knew him well:

> As if by magic he produced results under the most exacting circumstances. Now and then he came to Berlin to have his accounts approved. Everything was always perfectly in order. . . . Mannheimer solved continuously and elegantly all currency problems. It made him very rich. He was informed every day about the needs, the problems, the wishes and the instructions of the Reichsbank. . . . Mannheimer became one of the most potent bankers in Amsterdam, much disliked by Dutch bankers. He lived in luxury in a patrician house on the Heerengracht. He kept a substantial part of his fortune in gold bars in his cellar.[4]

After the war he became a very important but controversial personality in France where he resided regularly in a haughty château cultivating his relations with politicians. He even lent money to the government during a financial crisis. He died of a heart attack in August 1939. His currency speculations had turned against him; his bank had failed, leaving a debt of 42 million guilders.[5]

When the war ended and international trade resumed, European currencies started to depreciate against the dollar. During the war a highly disciplined German population had turned in the gold it possessed in exchange for paper Reichsmarks. The paper in circulation in 1918 was about five times its pre-war level. Prices, rigidly controlled by the government, had merely doubled. After the war the allies had ordered a blockade of the country which lasted nine months. As soon as the blockade ended, the superabundance of paper money caused a rapid rise in prices.

From mid-1921 onwards the depreciation of the German mark accelerated: the Reichsbank, the successive governments and the press explained that this was due to the reparations. In May 1921 the allies laid down an ultimatum demanding that Germany pay one billion gold marks in cash before the end of August. The demand was duly met, but the German government had to borrow about two-thirds of the sum from the Mendelssohn bank in Amsterdam, of which Mannheimer had become a partner. The loan was to be repaid before the end of the year and, as the British ambassador in Berlin observed, the operation had a considerable effect on the exchange rate of the mark.[6]

Economic activity remained high in Germany. The more rapid the rise in prices, the greater became the intensity of public demand for goods. Business boomed and people, expecting prices would continue to rise, were caught in a buyers' panic. The Reichsbank printed increasingly larger quantities of money, asserting that the paper inflation was not the cause but the consequence of the external depreciation of the mark, itself a result of reparations. No attempt could be made at any stabilization until a tolerable solution to the reparations problem had been found.

The depreciation of the currency created among certain classes of people a vested interest in its maintenance and continuation. Farmers whose property was mortgaged saw in it an opportunity to lighten their financial burden. Enterprising industrialists, through clever use of bank credits, were able to acquire factories from less astute owners and pay for them in depreciated marks. Some powerful industrialists came to regard with apprehension any increase in the value of the currency. They perceived the advantages of inflation and the profits it bestowed upon them: while prices were rising wages were kept down. The president of the Reichsbank himself, Rudolf Havenstein, whose legal and administrative background was inadequate for the responsibility he had been given, persisted in the belief that this was not inflation but a shortage of goods. He did not understand the complexities of the situation and, in addition, he lacked the determination and courage to resist pressures which were brought upon him.[7]

French public opinion became increasingly acrimonious, accusing the German government of deliberately allowing its finances to deteriorate in order to prove its inability to pay reparations. The war-weary French population, reluctant to make further sacrifices in the interest of indispensable reconstruction and divided within itself concerning the distribution of the fiscal burden, was united in the conviction that Germany should be forced to pay the full costs of reconstruction.[8]

The French government and the press reassured themselves by repeating endlessly: 'Germany will pay.' The tons of gold and the trainloads of merchandise Germany was going to send would relieve France of its economic and financial problems: the miracle was bound to happen.[9]

The Versailles Treaty was to remain the final verdict: Germany would be kept in lasting servitude, allowed only sufficient economic and financial potency to pay reparations to France.

In January 1923 French and Belgian troops invaded and occupied the Ruhr because insufficient quantities of coal had been delivered. Against British opposition, Poincaré decided that the army would stay there to protect a group of French and Belgian civilians responsible for the control of mine production.

The reaction was immediate. The German government organized the 'passive resistance' of the population: trains, mines, factories came to a standstill. All activities were halted. But the people had to subsist; the government continued to distribute paper money in ever increasing quantities. Before the war, the presses of the Reichsbank had printed all the banknotes. In 1923, 30 paper factories and 133 printing firms worked day and night to supply the money. Big industrial firms, while production was halted, printed their own notes to pay the workers. Municipalities printed notes valid only within their territory. These were for a while accepted in local shops. The population, supplied with more and more money and faced with the prospect of a rapidly disappearing supply of goods, besieged the shops until the shopkeepers refused to accept any more worthless paper and resorted to barter: a shabby cinema demanding two bricks of coal for admission to a performance, or a barber exchanging an egg for a haircut, were current practice.

In the heart of an ancient, orderly and highly organized civilization the money device went utterly to pieces. Fortunes disappeared. Lifetime savings of the middle class, their hope and future security, became worthless. The relations between debtor and creditor completely changed. Worthless money inflicted misery and famine upon millions. The few who had dollars or another stable foreign currency bought whatever they wanted amazingly cheaply. Foreigners swarmed into the country to buy anything of value. To most Germans money became a baffling and terrifying thing; the general dismay and confusion played into the hands of the few astute, able to foresee the consequences and the opportunities of inflation.

The fundamental canons of a well-ordered bourgeois society were shaken, not through the fault of the population but because of incomprehensible circumstances for which the government and the former enemies seemed responsible. A government of law and order was in power, expert bankers were supposed to be controlling the money supply. Yet the Great

Inflation had descended like a nightmare on the German people. A loaf of bread, when available, cost millions and later billions of marks. Hunger demonstrations shook many cities. Starvation and idleness caused food riots. Warehouses were plundered and people were shot. While in the cities children starved for lack of milk, peasants, refusing to accept worthless money, fed their surplus milk to the pigs. Groups of angry men swarmed into the countryside, attacked farms, killing cows and pigs.

The working class turned to Communism and for a while it seemed that the Communist party might grab power. The important Berlin newspaper *Germania* wrote on 27 July 1923: 'It is a situation for a dictator. The conditions call for a Mussolini in bullet-proof armour with a revolver in either hand.'

People who had access to foreign banknotes started hoarding them. Professional speculators, foreseeing a further depreciation of the mark, organized an active market, intent upon a continued rise of the dollar. Amidst the general calamity, a few people became very rich.

> German governments were often accused of having wanted the depreciation of the mark in order to show that it was impossible for Germany to pay reparations. . . . I cannot consider that accusation seriously. The accusation that the collapse of the German exchange was provoked by bold groups of speculators seems better founded. The objection to that is that speculation cannot be the original cause of the depreciation of the currency of a country. . . . Speculation appears when for certain reasons . . . the exchanges are unstable. Speculation weakens and eventually disappears when the causes which provoked the original depreciation of the currency become less. . . .
>
> The well-known movements of international speculators first fixed their abode in Vienna; later they passed to Berlin and after the German monetary reform they transferred their activities to Paris, where the situation of the French franc promised to open for them a field of further activities. Speculation often anticipated the future variations but exaggerated them, partly because its action was . . . reinforced by the operations of the public, who followed more or less blindly the example of the professional speculators.[10]

If the government had unconsciously caused and accelerated the inflation, many industrialists considered the depreciation as a necessary condition for industry to improve its productivity. The possibility of an increase in the value of the mark was viewed with apprehension: the industrialist Klöckner observed that 'the consequence would be a disaster of incredible magnitude'.

Another major industrialist, Hugo Stinnes, whose influence on the government was considerable, opposed a foreign loan because it would have raised the exchange rate of the mark to a level which the German economy could not endure.

> He has woven intrigues against every Government which he was afraid would put order in the internal conditions of Germany. . . . By means of credits amounting to milliards, whose value was continually reduced by inflation, he bought one firm after another in every branch of industry, he appropriated banks, financed shipping firms, acquired participations abroad and controlled numerous enterprises. And all this with the system of his politics, which aimed at the maintenance of inflation and disorder.[11]

The collapse of the mark was a shattering experience for millions of people. It caused profound helplessness and despair. The end of money meant the end of order and morality, of self-reliance and dignity. The truths which seemed most certain, the difference between good and evil, vanished before the eyes of the individual. A few people in a position to incur debts had discovered the diabolic magic of money and made fortunes amidst general wretchedness. It caused intense resentments and primitive hostilities. An eyewitness recounts:

> The state wiped out property, livelihood, personality, squeezed and pared down the individual, destroyed his faith in himself by destroying his property – or, worse: his faith and hope in property. Minds were ripe for the great destruction. The state broke the economic man beginning with the weakest. . . . From Russia the explosion of 1917 had resounded throughout the world. . . . Nowhere, with the exception of Russia, did the state destroy property as radically as in Germany. . . . While Stinnes, on his royal-industrial throne at Mühlheim on the Ruhr, calmly took it upon himself to destroy private property in Germany, Hitler stamped furiously back and forth on his platform in the ill-lit beer hall and shouted. . . . He spoke like a learned doctor of economics, and just this sounded quite incredible in his mouth. . . . The chaos should have been exploited for a transformation of the German economy. He censured the government, because 'when the soldiers streamed back from the front, it did not distribute to them much-needed projects (public works and housing), but sent them back to the places from which they had been called to the

colors'. . . . It was a decisive turn in Hitler's career when his friend and admirer Ernst Hanfstaengl, scion of an old-established and wealthy printer's family, himself half-American by descent, borrowed for him the fabulous sum of one thousand dollars. This money enabled Hitler to set up, in February 1923, the *Völkischer Beobachter* as a daily paper.[12]

Citizens numbering in millions, said Hitler, would die of hunger, because the farmer would stop selling his grain and butter for worthless billions. He set his hope in the 'revolt of the starving billionaires'.

He also vituperated against the 'Diktat' of Versailles and scolded the German people for its cowardice. When a French firing squad shot, in Düsseldorf, a patriotic German saboteur by the name of Schlageter, he became the hero of the National Socialist party. While the French were still in the Ruhr fomenting separatist movements, passive resistance ended on 26 September 1923, thus preparing the ground for the resumption of economic activity and for a stabilization of the mark.

On 20 November 1923, 12 days after Hitler's aborted *putsch* in Munich, the rate of exchange was 4.2 billion marks to a dollar. The pre-war rate had been 4.2 and it seemed that, for accounting reasons, it was the right time to stop inflation. Havenstein died that same day and Hjalmar Schacht became president of the Reichsbank. New banknotes called Rentenmarks were issued. One Rentenmark was worth one billion Reichsmarks.

The speculators did not believe that the Reichsbank would be able to hold this rate. They borrowed the new Rentenmarks to exchange against dollars in the free market. Immediately the Rentenmark price went up, but the public, satisfied that valid money was available again, did not follow. When the time for repayment came, the speculators were forced to sell their dollars at the official rate and lost money. By the end of the year the Rentenmarks and the Reichsmarks were accepted on equal terms.

Schacht acquired over the years a reputation as a wizard in national and international finance. He remarked later that the Reichsbank had had to overcome two enemies of stabilization: the speculators and the companies and municipalities which had printed their own money. Under this system 'everybody had his Reichsbank'. Shortly before the stabilization date he attended a meeting organized by the *OberbÜrgermeister* of Cologne where he had to face a very hostile crowd: all the participants, mainly the industrialists, wanted inflation to continue. Schacht concludes: 'It was proof again that a large assembly is unable to understand a given situation and can never decide upon a useful course of action.'[13]

To set the economy in motion industry needed credit and the only authority able to grant credit was the Reichsbank. By the end of March 1924, outstanding credits amounted to more than two billion marks, much of it being used to buy raw materials abroad. Once more the speculators began to hoard dollars. Instructions had been issued whereby foreign-exchange purchase orders were to be executed by the banks only if the full amount was deposited in marks. Several banks chose to ignore the instructions. They were immediately excluded from using the Reichsbank's clearing facilities and their bills were no longer discounted. The measure caused a great stir in the banking community, but it stopped speculation. Schacht noted:

> Understandably enough this intervention, which contradicted all traditions of central banking, caused a great outcry. The bank stood firm against this storm. . . . The bank's action saved not only the currency but also confidence in the currency. This confidence was not based on tedious expositions of proof or exhortations, but was supported by the weight of action.[14]

Stabilization of the mark brought stabilization of prices and of the whole economy. German industry was gripped by the urge to produce. The successive governments of the Weimar republic, controlled by coalitions of social-democrats and bourgeois conservatives, were moderate in outlook. They were struggling to rebuild the German economy and manoeuvred endlessly to stop or ease the reparations burden.

The former allies were deeply divided regarding the treatment to be given to Germany. When the British were called upon to repay their debt to the United States, they declared in 1922 that they would claim only enough to meet their American obligations. France considered Versailles the final verdict: Germany must be kept in lasting servitude in order to prevent another war, the only language the Germans understood and respected was force.

In order to resolve the differences, numerous conferences were held in an atmosphere of irritation and frustration; plans were put forward and adopted, pacts and treaties were signed and often repudiated, but without any constructive results. The major obstacle to peace in Europe was the reparations muddle and the governments were completely unable to agree on a practical and acceptable answer.

From a distance America watched these interminable quarrels in Europe where thousands of its men had died in a war that was of no concern to them. A recession had hit the country after the war and in 1922 the government had raised tariffs considerably to protect its producers against imports from low-wage countries. The policy of the United States would be to export and to collect debts from its former allies.

Finally the Morgan bank stepped in and suggested taking the problem out of politics, entrusting it to a group of financial experts and putting it on a strictly commercial basis. The proposal was accepted by all governments.

4 Morgan's Solution

In 1923, after numerous reparations conferences summoned by the League of Nations and several years of futile discussions, it became evident that no progress would be made because no common language could be found and no common course of action could be agreed upon.

Poincaré had decided on the occupation of the Ruhr, which had not been profitable; the earnings from seizures and forced deliveries came to less than the value France had been receiving before the occupation. But, as a result of the 'passive resistance', it had led to the collapse of the Reichsmark. A British member of the Reparations Commission remarked:

> It looked as if France was more interested in dismembering and ruining Germany than in collecting reparations and relations between the Allied governments grew more and more strained.[1]

A group of American bankers, headed by J. P. Morgan Jr, attending the conferences as observers, proposed to solve the reparations imbroglio by taking it out of politics and putting it on a financial basis.

The Allied Reparation Commission appointed a Chicago banker who had shuttled all his life between politics and finance, Charles G. Dawes, as president of the committee of experts to take on the problem. Dawes was a figurehead, the real power behind the idea being the Morgan bank. The British and French governments agreed to let an impartial committee of experts, working under the auspices of American banks, decide about Germany's ability to pay reparations and the manner in which they should be paid. The same banks which had, to a large extent, financed the war now stepped forward to take the situation in hand and clean up the quagmire created by the fumbles and failures of the governments. After a number of meetings, the Dawes Plan was accepted. It represented a compromise between economic feasibility and political demands, but it was a compromise whose findings were dominated by economic experts. The Dawes Plan, by transforming the reparations controversy into a technical problem of economics, would defuse wartime passions and pave the way for normal diplomatic relations. The Dawes Committee had stated clearly that it was concerned with business, not politics, and had carefully avoided any reference to the responsibility for German inflation. The nations entitled to reparations had initially filed claims amounting to 266 billion gold marks, but this figure was later halved.

The bankers were pictured by the press as independent and disinterested practical businessmen who would succeed where the politicians had failed. In the United States the Plan was considered as proof of the New World's ingenuity coming to the rescue of the Old.

Some of Morgan's competitors resented its claim to pre-eminence and its style of leadership. A syndicate of important United States banks would issue substantial quantities of German bonds to be purchased by the American public. The dollars would then be loaned to Germany for the restoration of its economy so that it could pay reparations.

The statute of the Reichsbank was modified to ensure its independence from political influence and a 33-year-old American banker, Parker Gilbert, was put in charge of a committee with the power to supervise a large section of German finances. Arrogant and irascible, he aroused considerable resentment in Berlin but he had to be tolerated. Under the direction of the Reichsbank the mark was maintained on a stable parity in relation to the dollar and an initial loan of $200 million was granted. As collateral for the loan the German railways and a substantial portion of industrial plant were mortgaged.

It seemed a very functional plan: nobody asked how the investors would foreclose and take possession of the property in case of default. The banks would merely take a commission. The interest and the reimbursement were due in dollars: the American public apparently did not ask how Germany would acquire enough dollars to pay interest and reimburse the capital. Keynes had warned:

> If bonds are issued in America on the analogy of American bonds issued in Europe during the nineteenth century, the analogy will be a false one; because, taken in the aggregate, there is no natural increase, no real sinking fund, out of which they can be repaid. The interest will be furnished out of new loans, so long as they are obtainable, and the financial structure will mount always higher, until it is not worth while to maintain any longer the illusion that it has foundations.[2]

Prompted by a massive advertising campaign and lured by high interest rates, the American public subscribed enthusiastically: in New York the sale of bonds was such a success that the lists had to be closed within a quarter of an hour of the opening. The yield of German bonds ranged over the years from $6\frac{3}{4}$ to 9 per cent compared with an average of 4 per cent in the domestic bond market. The Morgan bank was at the centre of this gigantic operation and nobody seemed to question its wisdom. Many years later Schacht noted:

> American and other foreign bankers granted Germany countless loans without properly investigating and evaluating the possibilities of repayment. The reason for granting these credits was not so much the endeavour to help the German economy to its feet after its defeat in war – it is well known that there is nothing cosy about money matters – but rather the profitable business of placing German loan issues on the American market. . . . A just verdict of these foreign loans would show that the responsibility of the lenders was at least as great if not greater than that of the borrowers. . . . While in New York in the autumn of 1925, I had the opportunity of alerting the American authorities to the dangers of granting too much credit to Germany. My efforts came to grief because the American bankers had an insatiable appetite for business, and continued to offer German borrowers new loans.[3]

As it later became evident, the bankers were only concerned with their underwriting profits and commissions and not with the safety of the money. It was not theirs. The massive advertising used to induce the American public to buy the bonds was followed by even more high-pressure salesmanship to persuade the Germans to take the loans.

Bank salesmen flocked all over Germany to persuade anybody willing to listen that they should borrow as many dollars as they wanted. Schacht observed that 'it was hardly possible to pass in front of the Adlon Hotel, Unter den Linden, without having some finance agent jump out, asking whether one did not know an industrial company or a municipality that might be willing to accept a loan'. A Bavarian hamlet discovered by American agents to be in need of about $125 000 was urged and finally persuaded to borrow $3 million.

The transfusion of credit had an extraordinary effect on the German economy. By the end of 1924 the Reichsbank had more foreign exchange than it needed although the German balance of payments was growing increasingly passive. Early in 1925 the commercial banks had more money than they knew what to do with. A large share of the money, instead of being invested by industry and put into productive channels, was used for public expenditure, mostly local: parks, swimming pools, theatres, and so on.[4]

With the dollars borrowed from the American public, Germany paid reparations to France and its allies who used the money to pay their war debts to the United Sates government. Under the Dawes Plan Germany 'made all payments fully and punctually as they came due'. Between 1925 and 1931, when a moratorium was announced, billions of dollars were sent to Germany never to come back.

During the ten years following the war, Germany had not produced any exportable surplus. With much of the borrowed money the Reichsbank had purchased gold. American and other investors punctually received interest on their bonds but the interest was paid from fresh loans. Over a period of five years, from 1924 until the crash of 1929, the American public bought about 13 billion dollars' worth of German bonds. The banks gave assurance that they had the resources for dealing with problems of 'transfers of capital'. Gradually some of the more perspicacious observers started wondering how long this could go on and whether serious problems would not arise when American lending ceased.

The Office of the Agent General for Reparations Payments was an international body consisting of the best financial and economic experts from many countries. It published annual reports containing a complete survey of every aspect of Germany's financial and economic situation. It never sounded a warning that the indebtedness of the country might some day cause serious problems when the avalanche of loans ceased.

Since Germany paid its debts, the tension between the former enemies had gradually abated. Unprecedented affluence radiated from the United States over many parts of the world. Increased production and consumption required more capital. Governments expanded the circulation of money and banks were available to trustworthy borrowers in need of funds.

In 1929 the Dawes Plan came to an end. By instituting control over German finances it was a constant source of irritation to German public opinion. It was replaced by a new plan headed by Owen D. Young, President of a Morgan affiliate. The Young Plan was to organize the liquidation of outstanding problems arising out of the war. The areas of Germany still occupied were to be evacuated.

In June 1929 the Young Committee decided to abandon the 'fantastic figure of 132 milliard marks' and to replace it by the payment of annuities over a period of 59 years, until 1988. A new institution, the Bank for International Settlements was set up in Basle to act as a trustee and administrator of the Reparations Plan. The board of directors consisted of the governors of the central banks of France, Britain, Germany, Italy, Belgium and Japan. The State Department forbidding Federal Reserve participation, American finance was represented directly by J. P. Morgan & Co.

There are two American directors in the Bank (against one each for the other countries) chosen by Morgan, and the president, another American, was chosen upon Morgan's advice. The House of Morgan dominates the Bank for International Settlements.[5]

For years the Germans called the Bank for International Settlements (BIS) the 'Morgan bank'. Although Germany had signed the agreement formally binding itself, in banking circles the Young Plan was dismissed as 'purely illusionary obsessions' and 'Jules Verne dreams'.

In the autumn of 1929 the Wall Street crash abruptly ended the willingness and the ability of the American public to buy German bonds. At the same time it became apparent that Germany would be unable to fulfil its obligations under the Young Plan.

Reparations payments came to a stop; the one-year moratorium granted in June 1931 at the instance of President Hoover could not prevent the total collapse of the German economy in 1931. A year later, all claims to further reparations were officially buried.

A few years later, Schacht was on a visit to Washington as president of the Reichsbank:

My discussions with the American president, Franklin Roosevelt and the foreign minister, Cordell Hull, in April, 1933, gave me the opportunity to acquaint them with the hopeless financial and political position in which Germany found itself. After a few discussions for which I had prepared my brief, I frankly explained to President Roosevelt in the presence of his foreign minister, Cordell Hull, and the German ambassador, Luther, that it would shortly become necessary to suspend for the time being all payment of interest on the loans granted to Germany. Roosevelt's reaction was quite astonishing. I had expected an indignant response, instead Roosevelt slapped his thighs and exclaimed laughingly 'Serves the damned Wall Street bankers right'. Naturally on the next day Cordell Hull handed me a letter which he had no doubt instigated himself, in which the President expressed himself as extremely shocked by my expositions.[6]

The American public, believing that the bonds and the interests were guaranteed, and lured by high returns, lost billions of dollars in the process.

In 1953 the United States and West Germany signed an agreement whereby, after reunification of the two separate states, the German government would resume paying interest on these bonds and repurchase them from their present owners. This agreement is currently being carried out.

5 The Crash

During the years from 1925 to 1929 the world seemed on its way to economic stability. By 1925 international trade and production had increased to very satisfactory levels; constant progress was made in most countries and the living standards gradually improved.

Britain was the exception. Winston Churchill had become Chancellor of the Exchequer; in his first Budget speech on 28 April 1925 he announced that Britain was returning to the gold standard at the prewar parity rate of $4.86 to the pound.

Lacking financial expertise, Churchill had willingly accepted the doctrine preached to him as an article of faith by the Treasury, the Bank of England and his own Cabinet colleagues: the return to gold meant an increase in the value of sterling against other currencies and the restoration of London as the world's principal money market. A return to 'normalcy' would enable the pound 'to look the dollar in the face' and bring renewed prestige to the City. Gold and the prewar parity were prescriptions for industrial prosperity and financial preeminence.

Few contradicted this theory; one of them was J. M. Keynes. In a prophetic pamphlet, *The Economic Consequences of Mr Churchill*, he asserted that the Chancellor had been misled by his advisers. But Conservative Britain accepted the eventuality of a painful depression of prices and wages, with the resulting stagnation and unemployment, just as in the nineteenth century. It soon became evident that the pound was overvalued and that the already hard-pressed British export industries would have to reduce their costs and scale down wages.

The miners were the first to taste the effects of the Chancellor's return to 'normalcy'. When the occupation of the Ruhr ended, the reopened mines had resumed production and a flood of German coal poured into the European markets, destroying the virtual monopoly Britain had briefly enjoyed. The mineowners immediately decided to slash wages by 10 to 25 per cent. The miners rejected the proposal and prepared to strike. The owners decided on a lockout. In support of the miners, a general strike hit the country; the miners' strike lasted until November 1926 when it was finally defeated, leaving deep bitterness. The return to the gold standard, 'the most decisively damaging action involving money in modern times',[1] was conceived and inspired by a central banker who considered himself and was considered as the greatest financial genius of his time, Montagu Norman. Churchill often said later it was the most serious mistake he ever made.[2]

The United States had reaped the profits of the war. It became a magnet for impoverished Europeans and the beacon of a new way of life: mass production, high wages, increasing profits, real estate speculation and stock market booms. The American nation had found the secret of permanent prosperity: rugged individualism unhampered by government interference and above all 'the character of the nation'.

Under President Coolidge there had been two 'bull markets' followed by the Florida real estate boom. It was God's intention that the Americans should be rich. Production and employment increased year after year; prices were relatively stable and wages were gradually going up. The production of cars swelled from 4.3 million in 1926 to 5.3 million in 1929. Business was good and getting better all the time and more people had more money than ever before. The bubble continued to grow unrelentingly: the Florida boom and other real estate ventures made people feel that it was easy to get rich quick on the stock market if they played it right. The secret was simple: borrow money to buy shares and watch their value increase – in other words: trade on margin.

For every share bought there was a share sold. But new shares were constantly thrown on the market and bought at ever increasing prices. Wise men who understood finance and who foresaw the future better than the general public, predicted an era of endless prosperity. Said President Coolidge: 'The main source of these unexampled blessings lies in the integrity and the character of the American people.'

In 1928 Hoover had been elected president and a 'victory boom' broke out on Wall Street. Industry profits increased as expected but soon the stock prices began to outpace the earnings. Speculators did not take notice of the trend and fever took hold of the American public. Since stock was increasingly bought on margin, banks started lending enormous sums for speculation. In 1927 loans to brokers carried interest rates ranging from 6 to 12 per cent – a very profitable business. Loans for buying securities on margin gradually increased and the trend continued through the summer of 1929.

Some became aware of the fact that a speculative boom is inherently self-liquidating. The Federal Reserve Board in Washington had issued a warning, over the objections of the New York Federal Reserve Banks against using Federal Reserve funds for speculation. The market had slightly quavered in response to the warning but soon recouped. Early in 1929 Charles Mitchell, head of the National City Bank, became director of the New York Federal Reserve. His bank, like the other large New York banks, had taken the lion's share of this lending spree; but as the orgy of unrestrained and unreasonable speculation became alarming, the banks increased the rate for carrying securities to 20 per cent. The market dropped on heavy selling. Mitchell immediately announced that the National City Bank was committing $25 million to brokers' loans and the market promptly recovered. Mitchell would later be found guilty of tax evasion and was sacked from the Federal Reserve.

At this stage, if the Federal Reserve had moved strongly to restrict lending for speculation, it would have been responsible not only for ending the boom but also for its consequences, a depression, meaning the loss of billions of dollars by hundreds of thousands of speculators who considered themselves prudent and deserving investors. The Federal Reserve chose to do nothing. It seemed wiser to let events take their course and thus allow events to take the blame. Paul Warburg, one of the most lucid and prestigious figures in the financial community, had warned against the unrestrained speculation: he was accused of 'sandbagging American prosperity'.

Wall Street's magic money machine had provided funds to anyone willing to buy securities. Billions of dollars were loaned, shares were bought and the money went back to the banks. In 1928 the market had a few hiccups but as long as share prices kept rising the boom gained momentum. When the increase slowed down or stopped, there was no point in holding shares bought with borrowed money.

So people started selling. Struck by panic, they sold day after day at constantly falling prices. The market continued to drop, rally and fall again. Then, suddenly, there were no more rallies. The cataclysmic break on Wednesday, 23 and Thursday, 24 October 1929 sent a shudder of apprehension through the country. The bottom seemed to fall out of the market. The following Tuesday it did. The plunge became terrifying, the collapse turning the Exchange into a frantic madhouse. The Depression had started. People and businesses went bankrupt, factories closed, causing massive unemployment, shattering the American dream. Millions of men lost their jobs, then their savings, their credit and finally their hope. They queued up in soup lines. Over 12 million people were unemployed without unemployment compensation. Provision for the poor, charity, was held to be a local responsibility. The tragedy of the Great Crash is that the collapse of artificial wealth – an overvalued stock market – caused the collapse of commodity prices and the ruin of agriculture and industry, of production and distribution. The Depression lasted until 1939, when the conflict with Germany forced Britain to turn to the United States for the purchase of war material.[3]

The crash was blamed on erroneous policies of the Federal Reserve and on the irresponsible greed of the banking community. It became apparent that a gullible public had become the victim of reckless bankers. The stereotype of bankers, as conservative men of impressive self-confidence, careful and responsible individuals, was shattered for years. Congressional investigations proved some to be incompetent, others outright crooked. Public sentiment against the large banks would take a long time to melt down.

In 1929, 659 banks failed; in 1930, 1352 closed and the following year there were 2294 bankruptcies. By the end of 1933 nearly half of the nation's banks had disappeared. The bankers were almost unanimously blamed for the Depression. Franklin Roosevelt had waged his campaign partly on a platform directed against them. In his Inaugural Address on 4 March 1933 the new President said:

> Plenty is at our doorstep, but a generous use of it languishes in the very sight of supply. Primarily this is because the rulers of the exchange of mankind's goods have failed through their own stubbornness and their own incompetence, have admitted their failure and have abdicated. Practices of the unscrupulous money changers stand indicted in the court of public opinion, rejected by the hearts and minds of men. . . . The money changers have fled from their high seats in the temple of our civilization. We may now restore that temple to the ancient truths.

Two days later he issued an Executive Order closing all banks. Congress gave the President wide powers over the nation's monetary policies, national and international. To prevent speculation, banks were not permitted to engage in transactions in foreign exchange unless 'undertaken for legitimate and normal business requirements'.

Banknotes were still in use, but deposits amounting to billions of dollars had vanished as a result of the bank failures. It was a new and terrible experience; nothing in past history indicated what could or should be done; despite the crying need, no remedy was in sight. During the Depression the surviving banks had reserves but no customers. The Federal Reserve could make money available but it could not induce people to borrow.

President Roosevelt's address had somehow lifted the nation out of its state of shock. 'No one would ever know how close we were to collapse and revolution,' General Hugh S. Johnson later said. 'We could have got a dictator easier than Germany got Hitler.' Roosevelt's adviser R. Tugwell noted: 'I do not think it is too much to say that on March 4 we were confronted with a choice between an orderly revolution – a peaceful and rapid departure from past concepts – and a violent and disorderly overthrow of the whole capitalist structure.' Walter Lippmann wrote: 'At the end of February we were a congeries of disorderly panic-stricken mobs and factions . . . we became again an organized nation confident of our power to provide for our own security and to control our destiny.'

The economic Right disagreed:

> The hard-boiled businessman sums it up: 'Of course, many of our foreign loans later turned sour, and investors lost their money, but while we are shipping goods abroad, jobs are created. It doesn't matter, as far as current jobs and prices in the twenties are concerned, whether 10 years later the loans will turn out good or bad or whether they represent public or private gifts.' Or, as Leon Fraser, who used to be president of J. P. Morgan's First National Bank of New York, put it: 'It is better to have lent and lost than never to have lent at all.'[4]

THE DEPRESSION SPREADS TO EUROPE

One immediate effect of the Wall Street stock exchange crash of 1929 was suddenly to put an end to the willingness and the ability of the American banks and of the public to grant loans to Germany. In the summer of 1931 several of the largest German banks closed, precipitating the country in to a financial crisis. The government prohibited the export of capital. The Brüning coalition, faced with a sudden contraction of tax revenues, imposed a drastic reduction of public expenses, an increase in taxes as well as a general diminution in official wages and social security benefits.

These sudden 'famine laws' clamped down for no comprehensible reason on a hard-working and prosperous nation; they thunderblasted the German people for the second time in less than a decade. In January 1930 there were 3.2 million unemployed; in January 1931, 4.9 million; in February 1932, they were 6.1 million.

Germany had lived under the tutelage of the American bankers who had sold billions of dollars of bonds. The country had borrowed abroad far more than it had paid in reparations. Germany had paid France, France had paid Britain and also the United States while Britain in turn had paid the United States. The dollars lent by the American public were paid back to the American Treasury.

The German crisis of 1931 started in the manner of the classical financial crises of the nineteenth century. On 11 May 1931 the Creditanstalt, one of the most powerful banks on the Continent, controlling about 75 per cent of Austria's industrial resources, was declared insolvent. Founded by the house of Rothschild in 1855, it had obtained large credits from numerous banks in the United States and Europe. When it collapsed, these banks saw their credits frozen. The Habsburg empire had been dissected after the war: Austrian industry had lost its traditional markets and become unviable. The Creditanstalt's investments had gradually dwindled away. A projected loan to the Austrian government had been made impossible because France insisted on a renunciation of Austria's proposed customs union with Germany as a condition of the loan.

Soon Austria's difficulties spread to Germany: a run on the German banks began at the end of May. The German banks had for years offered high interest rates to attract foreign deposits; by tradition they are 'universal' banks and much of these funds had been supplied to industry as long-term capital. This made the banks very vulnerable, since most of the capital was uncallable in the case of an emergency.

President Hoover offered Europe the opportunity to check the slide; he proposed a one-year moratorium on all payments on inter-governmental debts. France refused. On 18 July *The New Statesman and Nation* reviewed the situation:

The fate of Germany – and of the rest of us – is still in the balance. Hope succeeds fear, and fear hope, almost from hour to hour. . . . The danger is that France may continue to prefer the risk of a weak, revolutionary and exasperated Germany to the danger of a reconstructed and free Germany. . . . Without French cooperation, without the assurance that the debt problem would be more than momentarily solved, further help for Germany seems only to be throwing good money after bad. But without that help the Brüning government cannot last for long. And a Fascist-Nationalist successor would be another blow at all our plans and projects for international reconstruction. The tragedy is that the overwhelming majority of Europeans and Americans are agreed in wishing to cut through this barb-wire entanglement of international indebtedness. They have learnt, as economic men, that there are some debts which it is neither blessed to give nor to receive. But as political men, in their petty nationalism, they imposed this burden on Germany and they have waited too long to admit their folly. And always in the background there is the shadow of the coming Disarmament Conference – the last opportunity, as we all know, of disarming Europe before Germany asserts her power to rearm.

France refused to give in. The argument dragged on and after a few more unsuccessful attempts to secure further credits, Germany's reserves were exhausted. Then the failure of the largest textile firm, Nordwolle, forced the Danat bank to suspend payments. American and European banks rushed in to withdraw their deposits; the American public tried to sell as many German bonds as it could. Within six weeks Germany had to absorb one billion dollars' worth of these securities. The German government suspended foreign payments and issued emergency decrees limiting withdrawals and imposing exchange controls. Germany's difficulties affected its creditors, everyone trying to repatriate as many assets as possible, hell-bent on strengthening personal liquidity. In a scramble for gold, the French government withdrew from London whatever balances it could. Sterling exchanges fell below the gold point; the heavy outflow of gold obstinately failed to produce a recovery in sterling. Despite attempts to secure further credits, withdrawals and speculation continued to weaken the pound.

Early in September 1931 Prime Minister MacDonald told Parliament: 'It is our duty to remain here, and it is your duty to keep us here, until the crisis has passed, until the world is convinced once again that sterling is unassailable.'[5] On Monday, 21 September, a bill suspending the gold standard was rushed through Parliament. A former Labour minister is said to have commented: 'They never told us we could do that.'[6]

Thirty years later, reviewing the sad, mad story of 1931, *The Economist* wondered if it could happen again:

> If a country were carrying two million unemployed it would be much less frightened nowadays of letting its exchange rate depreciate; a large part of the fears that swayed Britain thirty years ago were based on a complete misunderstanding of what had happened in Germany in 1922–23. And, however small the reforms in world liquidity so far, there has been an obvious change in international financial attitudes too; if a country reached the stage of Britain in 1931, the IMF would quickly mobilise large stand-by funds to support it instead of leaving one of the world's major trading nations at the mercy of a purely commercial calculation by Messrs J. P. Morgan.[7]

GERMANY AT THE CROSSROADS

The history of the period between the end of 1929 and Hitler's rise to power in 1933 has been generally distorted by the blind hatreds, biases and understandable prejudices of historians and commentators; this has produced a clichéd picture of the events and circumstances which made the German people abandon its faith in democracy.

The eyewitness documents of the time, written by people who did not know what would happen years later, render a picture very different from the propagated stereotyped analysis. For the sake of historical truth, these things must not be glossed over: blurring historical events is too common a practice.

The ravage wrought by the Wall Street crash hit Germany much more directly than any other European country: Germany's short-lived prosperity had been fuelled by foreign capital, mainly American. The German economy had been fed for five years by foreign loans; traditional German industriousness had made the country prosperous. The lending stopped abruptly and the foreigners withdrew their funds.

Without credits, factories suddenly ground to a halt. The nation had not yet completely recovered from the great inflation of 1923. The Communist vote steadily increased; the middle classes, who knew what had happened in Russia, looked desperately for someone to protect them against Bolshevism. Hitler promised 'work and bread', and full employment by organizing huge construction works, public and private, all over the country. He also promised social services, leisure time, maternal and family welfare. The system of liberal capitalism was condemned; only a planned economy would solve the gigantic problems facing the country. The obvious inability of the parliamentary regime to find an answer to these problems led a growing segment of the population to believe that an authoritarian regime was not only necessary but desirable. Until the middle of 1936, after he had been in power for three years, Hitler did not concern himself with the economic preconditions for waging a war.

He owed his rise to power to the despair of the unemployed proletariat, the academic youth unjustly deprived of their future, the businessmen and craftsmen threatened with bankruptcy and the farmers suffering from the fall in agricultural prices. Brüning's deflationary policy ended up in final bankruptcy when it threw six and a half million people out of work.

In June 1931 an English visitor to Germany observed:

What a different picture from that which I had brought home with me from my last visit to Berlin, three years ago. . . . There are also many police and beggars in the streets. . . . In Berlin, such slums as disfigure London and New York have always been unknown. . . . In Berlin today men's souls, in all classes and in all walks of life, are troubled to their depths . . . the doubt and gloom of foreboding which reign over his thoughts and feelings, strikes the foreign observer at every turn; and it is just in this contrast that the danger lies. For a people which has created this clean and orderly and upstanding city will not acquiesce tamely in a state of pauperism and idleness from which it can see now no prospect of redeeming itself by hard work and efficiency. The contrast, and conflict between the Prussian tradition, externalised in the streets and buildings of Berlin, and the present plight of the German people, breeds a state of mind which, short of the intervention of some *deus ex machina*, can only lead to revolution. . . .

The Government are . . . taking draconian measures to keep the public economy and the public finances of Germany sound. But these measures are all taken at the private individual's expense in the form of drastic rationalisation, which swells the ranks of the unemployed in the middle class as well as in the working class; drastic reductions of unemployment benefits (already startlingly low on English standards) and of official salaries. The fear is that, at the sharp touch of next winter, the individual may be goaded into political revolt against the personal economic sacrifices that are being demanded of him by the State . . . the young men of all classes in Germany are in a revolutionary frame of mind. . . . The higher the class, the greater the technical qualifications, the deeper the disillusionment. And, accordingly, the majority of people in Germany – and I believe it is still a majority – which dreads revolution is particularly afraid of the 'Akademiker', the young men who have been through the universities to qualify as doctors and lawyers and engineers, to find themselves stranded as an unemployed intellectual proletariat. These, one hears, will be the spearhead of the revolution – as Hitlerites to-day, as Communists to-morrow, but as revolutionaries day in and day out. They are revolutionaries not because they believe that this revolutionary programme or that will bring them salvation (for that matter all these programmes are remarkably vague) but because they are frustrated and disillusioned in their own individual lives. The spur that goads them is emotional and irrational. 'Life has misused us! We will hit back at life wherever we can see a target; hit back at the Government, the capitalists, the Jews, the foreigners. We cannot make our own position worse, and by some miracle we may make it better. At least we shall enjoy the satisfaction of relieving our feelings! At the worst we shall perish out of a world which has given us nothing to live and work for.'[8]

A majority of the people still hoped that a democratic government could solve their problems, but their number was rapidly diminishing: the obvious inefficiency of the parliamentary government in the face of the growing depression, even when it used decrees, made people believe that an authoritarian regime would be better equipped to solve their problems. In September 1930, after a few months of depression, the National Socialists had increased their number of seats in the Reichstag from 12 to 107, against 133 for the Social Democrats and 77 for the Communists.

There was still hope: early in August the National Socialists and the Communists had been defeated in the Prussian elections, but nearly ten million votes had been cast against Chancellor Brüning. *The New Statesman and Nation* observed: 'Germany gives us another chance'.

British newspapers hail the result as a victory for 'common sense' and 'sanity'. So it may be if we use our reprieve in a sane and common-sense way. The Paris press rejoices to find that pressure can still be put upon Germany without driving her to extremes. But the extremist parties only failed by a kind of accident which is unlikely to be repeated. If the policy advocated in the *Temps* and more violently in the *Journal des Débats* and *Ordre* wins in Paris, the policy of extremes will also win in Berlin. . . . We ought to be much more surprised than we are that a German revolution is again staved off. No people are so law-abiding or so patient. When the history of the last twelve years comes to be written we shall see that the central tragedy has been the failure to make use of the pacific mood of post-war Germany. For years after the war Germany was not only disarmed but she did not want to re-arm. The Hohenzollerns, the Junkers, the whole paraphernalia of Prussian militarism, were utterly discredited, and if the Allies had made different use of their victory, the endless chain of Franco-German hostility – war, revenge, and revenge again – would have been broken. The German universities were filled with sincere pacifists, anxious not for revanche but for a new kind of understanding, a new kind of Europe.

First, there were the crushing humiliations of Versailles, based on the obvious lie that the whole 'war guilt' was on Germany's shoulders, the surrender of German territory, east and west, the loss of her colonies. Then followed the black troops on the Rhine – the kind of savage incident that the aggressor thinks trivial and that the humiliated nation never forgets. Then the invasion of the Ruhr, the continuous struggle over reparations and the running sore of the Polish corridor, the opposition to German entry into the League – was any opportunity missed . . . to outrage German pride and evoke German nationalism, to make pacifism impossible? . . . We are apt to forget that the German people have lived for years on end with the flash of French bayonets in their eyes.[9]

The differences between the British and French positions were once more made clear at the London Conference on 20 July 1931. Prime Minister MacDonald had declared: 'We are not here to enforce or to defeat or to humiliate; we are here to understand, to consider our problems objectively, to consider how closely in essentials we depend upon each other.' Contrast with this the statement reportedly made by the French Defence Minister Maginot: 'We are not a conquered people but conquerors. Let the bellicose countries be silent. No capitulation to Germany. Let us defend our gold. As for our military power, I answer for it!'[10]

6 The Wasted Years

The Wall Street crash had destroyed the foundations of the international economic order. During the 1920s, despite the vicious circle of reparations, war debts and high tariffs, a satisfactory level of living standards had been achieved in most countries; world trade had continued to grow year after year.

The Depression triggered off a drastic reduction of international trade. In the early 1930s an unprecedented wave of exchange depreciations hit one currency after another. Most governments were averse to floating exchanges: they preferred to devalue when they felt compelled to do so for competitive reasons, in order to gain a larger share of the international market. Trade union power and the rise of socialism made a reduction in money wages – which had been current practice in Europe during the nineteenth century – unenforceable in most countries.

The decision by the British mineowners to reduce wages because the return to the gold standard had made their coal too expensive in the export market caused the miners' strike of May–November 1926. When the country went off gold in 1931 and let the pound float downwards, the benefits of lower export prices came to be appreciated. It did not take long, however, before businessmen discovered the inconvenience of fluctuating currency rates. *The Economist* observed:

Every trader in this country is conscious of the handicap which the fluctuating pound is putting in the way of international business; and if there is one objective of policy on which all would agree, it is that one of the most important interests of this country is to restore the utmost amount of stability to the international exchanges as quickly as possible.[1]

In Germany, Brüning's deflationary policy implying a drastic reduction of government spending and wage cutbacks had inflicted misery and despair.

The epidemic of devaluations started in the latter part of 1929 in agricultural countries such as Australia, New Zealand, Argentina and Brazil, which had in the past used this instrument during the recurrent cyclical depressions, when food prices suddenly declined. Organized destruction of food crops was common practice in these areas.

Agricultural countries encumbered with unsaleable stocks suffered a disastrous reduction in their purchasing power. Manufacturing countries were burdened with a mass of unemployed workers. In the midst of a superabundance of raw materials and consumer goods, this was a period of privation and depression. Credit provided by the banks was cheap, but money was lying idle. The spirit of enterprise had been strangled. The economic machine was completely out of gear; it seemed the ailment was hard to diagnose and the prescription difficult to find.

Keynes' suggestion was to 'spend magnificently'. But the men in power preferred to pursue 'a reduction of costs, a retrenchment in wages and a reduction of unproductive state expenditure'.[2] When Keynes published his *General Theory*, most reviewers found the book unsubstantiated. In conservative government and business circles a cut in real wages was generally considered sufficient to restore an adequate margin of profits and to reduce unemployment. Unions obviously resisted. Hence social strife flared up everywhere.

The United States owned about two-thirds of the world's gold reserves. President Roosevelt's financial advisers told him that a devaluation, a reduction of the gold value of the dollar, would have two sure and salubrious effects: it would raise the level of prices and restore the balance between the prices of raw materials and of consumer goods. Many professional economists considered that a depression was simply the result of a collapse in prices. Several European countries had devalued and gained a temporary advantage over the United States, still wedded to orthodoxy.

In March 1933 the President had suspended the export of gold except by licence from the Treasury. At once the value of the dollar began to sag abroad. Early in April, when the banking system was awakening from its coma of moratorium, all private gold holdings in the United States had been nationalized. The former parity of the dollar was abandoned and the currency was left to find its own level in the foreign-exchange market. Shortly before the start of the London Economic Conference, which Roosevelt had boycotted, a burst of speculation sent the dollar down. In two days, at the end of June 1933, it lost 5 per cent against the pound, making a fall of 25 per cent within a period of two months.

Convinced that 'the sound internal economic system of a Nation is a greater factor in its well-being than the price of its currency', Roosevelt decided that the government would buy gold in the open market and push its price up.

Every morning, beginning October 25, Morgenthau, Warren and Jesse Jones met in the President's bedroom to set the price of gold for the day. . . . The price that the morning conference established on any day made very little difference. The object was simply to keep the trend moving gradually upward, a little above the world price in the expectation that commodity prices would follow. . . . Roosevelt stuck close to his plan, but small deviations from his original estimates left him on Friday, November 3, with a range of from 19 to 22 cents to add to the price of gold – the original estimate had been 20 cents. The President that day took one look at Morgenthau, who was feeling more than usually worried about the state of the world, and suggested a rise of 21 cents. 'It's a lucky number,' Roosevelt said with a laugh, 'because it's three times seven.' Morgenthau later noted in his diary: 'If anybody really knew how we set the gold price through a combination of lucky numbers, etc, I think they would be frightened.'[3]

At the end of January 1934 the dollar price of gold was fixed at $35 an ounce. It would remain unchanged for almost four decades.

The suspension of the gold standard in Britain was followed by the devaluation of many currencies, most of which were later pegged to sterling. The dollar devaluation led to exchange depreciation in a large group of countries, mainly in Latin America.

At the end of 1936 the parities between the principal currencies were not very different from what they had been in 1930. Devaluations had been regarded primarily as a means of improving the country's foreign trade balance and as a result its volume of domestic employment; a relatively effective means in the short run, but one that necessarily operated at the expense of other nations and invited retaliation.

The action of the various governments was completely uncoordinated in time as well as in degree. The Tripartite Agreement of 1936 was an attempt to stabilize major currencies by international cooperation. In August 1936 France suffered another serious loss of gold. The Popular-Front government's decision to increase wages substantially, to grant paid vacations and other benefits to the workers, resulted in a sudden increase of French prices, making a new devaluation urgent. In order to avoid a repetition of the devaluation cycle, the French government asked the United States and Britain to maintain their rates and allow France to devalue. The Banque de France – a private institution – suggested a cooperation with the Bank of England and the Federal Reserve. But Roosevelt wanted to eliminate the central banks as primary decision-makers in international monetary relations. The three Treasuries, he said, should manage their currencies. This was more than a matter of vocabulary. It emphasized Roosevelt's conviction, and Morgenthau's, that monetary policy was the prerogative of government, not of private finance.[4]

The Tripartite Agreement was finally signed between the United States, Britain and France: the three countries would maintain the parity of their currencies through a Stabilization Fund. The agreement immediately won general applause. Switzerland, Holland, Belgium and Italy quickly announced their adherence to its principles and soon after officially joined the 'currency club'.

> On Saturday, September 26, the day after the announcement of the Tripartite Pact, Morgenthau had to use the Stabilization Fund to sustain the value of the pound. The markets in London and Paris were closed when sterling fell to $4.94 in New York. Morgenthau did not want sterling to close low, for that would make it seem as if the Treasury, in spite of the Tripartite Agreement, either could not or would not control fluctuations of exchange. He therefore immediately instructed the New York Federal Reserve Bank to buy $1 000 000 worth of sterling.[5]

The Federal Reserve reported that the Russian government wanted to sell £1 million at the best price and the Chase National Bank was handling the sale. Morgenthau was upset and directed the Federal Reserve to buy up the entire amount. 'They are trying to break down this agreement and I am calling the President and I will ask him whether I can give this out publicly,' he said. At a press conference he described what happened. The following day, Winthrop Aldrich, president of the Chase National Bank, called Morgenthau and insisted that this was perfectly ordinary business because Russia had to pay Sweden and needed dollars. Morgenthau considered that the Russians could perfectly well have used pounds to pay the Swedes. He never forgot the incident. Referring to Aldrich, he said one day: 'When you're John D. Rockefeller's brother-in-law you can afford to be stupid.'

THE CURRENCY SPECULATORS

Before 1914, under the gold standard, the profits to be made in foreign exchange were very small and speculation was confined to limited circles of professionals. After the war, when currencies were allowed to float, the struggle between the authorities trying to maintain currency stability and the speculators trying to upset this stability wherever they could, was a recurrent phenomenon; the centre of speculative bouts moved from country to country depending on circumstances. The debilitating consequences were obvious. *The Economist* commented:

> The suggestion has recently been voiced in *The Times* that combined international action should be taken against 'financial piracy', that is, against speculators attacking our currencies.[6]

Throughout the devaluation cycle of the 1930s the influence of speculative capital was considerable. Whenever the possibility of a devaluation in any country came under discussion, a flight of capital would develop, accentuating the depreciation and making the devaluation more probable. Usually, once the devaluation had been accomplished, the volatile funds were repatriated.

Gold was still used for the ultimate settlement of exchange differences between central banks. The problem of 'hot money', the migration of speculative funds, became the main cause of gold movements from one Exchange Fund to another. A country might find itself gaining or losing gold for reasons quite unconnected with its external trade balance, or with the general state of its industry, commerce or finance.[7]

Whereas the movement of goods was hampered by protectionist devices, the movement of capital generally remained free. In France the strife between Left and Right caused a number of financial crises. A shiver of alarm pervaded the French capitalists at the continual reiteration by the Socialists that when they came to power they would take the money where they found it. Holders of liquid credit transferred their funds from one currency to another, sometimes out of anxiety for the safety of their money, sometimes in the hope of snatching an easy profit and often to serve a political purpose, rocking the exchanges in order to discredit a government they did not like.

When the Popular Front came to power it put the Banque de France under a layer of government influence; it prohibited the export of gold but forgot to close some loopholes: French capitalists exported francs to the United States and exchanged them for dollars; the United States authorities then sent the francs back to France in exchange for gold.

Currency disturbances played havoc with the prices of internationally traded commodities. They created a new element of risk against which it was possible in many circumstances to take insurance by hedging, which, however, added to the cost. They involved constant and disturbing shifts of labour and resources between production for the home market and production for export. Experience also showed that fluctuating exchange rates did not promote adjustment, but were liable to generate anticipations of a further movement in the same direction, giving rise to speculative capital transfers which accentuated the disequilibrium.

The stability of exchange rates came to be considered essential, not only for international trade but for domestic stability as well, which did not mean that they should be permanently fixed. But any adjustment should be made by mutual consultation. Capital flight disrupted the monetary systems of the countries from which the capital fled and of the countries to which it fled. Capital flight was a reflection of the instability of exchanges and in turn was an important factor in adding to this instability. While in the early 1930s capital flight was very largely motivated by the hope of speculative profit, in the later thirties it was amplified by the refugees fleeing Nazi Germany.

THE TARIFF WARFARE

After the war the United States pursued a policy of high tariff walls, while promoting exports and collecting war debts. In 1920 the average United States tariff amounted to 16 per cent; by 1930 it had been increased to about 55 per cent. In 1930 President Hoover, giving in to the clamour of farmers and industry, signed the Smoot-Hawley Tariff Act. It seemed that the best way to combat depression was to reduce imports in order to provide work for the American unemployed. By 1938 the number of unemployed had increased to 12 million, an indication that the policy was not effective. The other countries considered the sudden substantial increase of American customs duties as an act of economic warfare and retaliated with tariffs, quotas and preferential agreements.

In February 1932 Britain, breaking with its free trade tradition, decided to keep out foreign goods. The Import Duties Act received the royal assent, and introduced a variety of protectionist measures: agricultural quotas, subsidies, exchange restrictions, bilateral clearing agreements and so on. The direct effects were limited, but the Act had a considerable impact on other countries' strategy in international trade. In August 1932 the Ottawa Conference reinforced Imperial Preference at the expense of non-British competitors; for years a major American bugbear, it was considered a weapon of offence against other countries' trade with the Commonwealth and was resented less for its effects than for the tone in which it was presented.[8]

Each tariff, each trade restriction had a psychological impact on other countries and intensified the disruption of foreign trade. Starting in

1936, Britain concluded clearing agreements with several countries, including Spain, Italy and Turkey. It was also announced early in May 1939 that the government had decided to accept the United States' proposal for negotiations to exchange the American surplus supplies of wheat and cotton against rubber and tin on a barter basis.[9]

Home markets turned into closed preserves for home producers, both agricultural and industrial. The isolated, divergent and contradictory measures by which each country attempted to protect itself and push off the burden to its trading partners, precipitated the crisis, rendering it more grievous for all. The struggle for a share of shrinking world trade and the mutually destructive rivalry induced each nation to adopt policies destined to protect itself, thereby causing world trade to shrink even further.

In several European countries one finance minister followed the other, in the hope that by trial and error a financial Messiah would reveal the secret for delivering the country of its afflictions. They were usually out of office before they could accomplish anything, leaving the responsibility to their successor. *The Economist* observed:

> Of all obstacles to international trade there are none more harmful and more formidable than those which arise either from monetary disturbances or from restrictions regarding the transfer of capital or of commercial payments. Sudden or violent variations in the mutual relation of currencies are liable to interrupt the normal currents of trade and to cause financial movements along abnormal channels ('hot money') while internal prices are adapting themselves to the new monetary parity. Uncertainty in this sphere is a very grave impediment to the conclusion of business or credit operations.[10]

Some countries were unable to sell their products while others tried at great cost to develop substitute materials and to live in economic isolation. By 1938 only the boom in armaments gave an appearance of activity to world trade. Many countries purchased supplies and raw materials for storage in view of the impending threat of war.

From then on suggestions for economic change were evaluated from the angle of war psychology and not for their intrinsic merits. It became ever more difficult to find a way of reversing the rising tide of brute force. Germany, in need of raw materials, claimed restitution of its former colonies. The United States resented preference systems and the failure to settle the war debts. It seemed impossible to liquidate the past; the interplay of economic and political developments, national and international, nurtured suspicion and rancour.

While the democracies, faced with the perennial disarray of public finances and governed by opposing factions, often forced to postpone desirable measures, tended to follow the precepts of traditional finance, the totalitarian states introduced new and untried methods. Mussolini, fed up with currency disturbances, simply prohibited the publication of financial news that might be of use to speculators.

Germany was a special case in the tariff war. As soon as Hitler came to power a vast programme of public works had been started: roads, tunnels, canals and dykes were a source of employment. Houses, factories and industrial equipment were repaired. The immense machinery of coercion through party organization made it possible to achieve results where a parliamentary system would have failed.

Many of the former unemployed were now in uniform. The Reichsbank granted direct credits to national and local authorities to carry out these activities. By 1934 armaments were included. In 1937 full employment had nearly been achieved and factories were looking for qualified workers. The German entrepreneurial spirit, helped by the close cooperation between industry and the universities, the diligence and discipline of its work force had completely transformed the economy. Chemistry and agriculture made astounding advances with the declared goal of national autarky, resulting in isolation and estrangement.

Shortly after coming to power, Hitler called Schacht back to the presidency of the Reichsbank. Proud of his ability to achieve results by discarding the dictates of traditional orthodox finance and of accepted economic theories, Schacht declared that gold was unnecessary and that the value of money was based on work. Balancing the budget, a difficult task for most governments, was a superfluous concern. 'Work creation' was the overriding purpose of government policy. Money and credit must be made available for legitimate demands, serving the national interest. The Reichsbank would provide the funds required to start the enormous public works programme. The effect was spectacular. Unemployment was virtually eliminated and in 1937 a shortage of raw materials affected the housing construction. The unemployment problem had been solved before Keynes finished explaining its causes.

The methods used in international trade were equally unusual. Shortly after the devaluation of the dollar, Germany announced that the mark would not be devalued. Devaluation was unthinkable: it was too closely associated in the mind of the German people with inflation, the memory of which continued to weigh like a nightmare. Germany established a number of bilateral clearing agreements with other countries in which the value of each currency was stipulated. No money was needed for international trade: goods would be exchanged against goods. To the amazement of experts in other countries, the German negotiators always insisted on keeping the value of the Reichsmark at a high level. Having solved its unemployment problem, Germany simply wanted to import as much as possible in exchange for the least possible exports.

These methods set the world's nerves on edge, but against the ingenuity of the devices developed by Schacht and his advisers, the techniques used by other countries were unavailing. Buying up the whole agricultural export surplus of some Eastern European countries at a higher price than the world market, Germany gradually established a practical monopoly over their exports. These countries soon found out that they could use the marks only for German goods but their economies were not organized to take them as the credits became available. Thus they piled up 'blocked marks'.

Schacht also instituted a system of subsidies in order to allow certain German exporters to compete in world markets. In 1936 there were more than a dozen different types of marks, some officially called 'credit balances' or 'accounts', but in reality marks of different values and for different use. Foreign trade became completely subjected to government decision, although the government did not own the goods.

An unending flood of laws, ordinances, decrees, restrictions, prohibitions and menaces regulated all foreign transactions. All this was a makeshift, the outcome of enforced and piecemeal adaptations to the exigencies of the day, and completely at variance with the policies of any other country. The rigid controls ensured that the scheduled supply of materials for military use would take precedence over industrial goods. Some of the measures taken shocked world opinion: in November 1936 a decree-law made it an offence punishable by death for a German citizen to move property – including money – out of Germany or even to move it from one foreign country to another, without declaring the whereabouts.[11]

In 1936 a dispute developed between Germany and the United States as a result of the German system of granting subsidies to exporters. This arrangement ran counter to the American anti-dumping legislation, and the United States not only imposed countervailing duties ranging up to 56 per cent, but required German exporters, under pain of forfeiture of the goods, to disclose the amount of subsidies. Under German law this constituted a serious offence. The German government prohibited all trade on a compensation basis between the two countries, which practically reduced trade to zero.[12]

By controlling exports and imports, the German government virtually determined the trade balance in advance. Schacht's inventive genius seemed indefatigable in devising new uses for the exchange clearing system by tricks which allowed the German government to import goods without having to pay for them.

Some Danubian and Balkan countries, in order to liquidate their blocked accounts, bought manufactured goods far in excess of what their population could absorb; moreover, they could only choose between a limited number of products: Rumania bought tens of thousands of typewriters, Greece an enormous number of harmonicas; Yugoslavia imported huge quantities of Aspirin and so on. But even Schacht's ingenuity and trickery could not keep up with the growing needs of the Nazi regime. As early as December 1936 Germany had advised Rumania that it was compelled to default on its current commitments; the only way to liquidate its debt was to sell obsolete German war material.[13]

The most subtle device may be described as a long-term credit trick. Anxious to safeguard themselves against unbalanced trade, Germany's trade partners had demanded that imports and exports be balanced. Germany agreed to import wheat, which had to be paid for in cash, and to export industrial equipment on a long-term credit basis. Since the clearing accounts had to balance and since Germany needed a few years to manufacture the capital goods, the wheat growers had in the meantime to be paid by their own governments.[14]

On 7 January 1939 Schacht advised Hitler that Germany was at the end of its reserves and that the deficit of the balance of payments was increasing alarmingly. Hitler's rearmament took up too much of the productive capacity. He also recommended strong action to prevent an acceleration of inflation caused by overemployment and by the sharply increased volume of banknotes the Reichsbank had been forced to issue. He was fired on the spot and was replaced by Walter Funk, which meant that Hitler alone would decide in future about Germany's monetary policy.[15]

World peace now depended on the decision of one man holding enormous masses of armed men in obedience, while the smaller countries became pawns in the confrontation between the Big Powers.

On 6 October 1939, shortly after the end of the Polish campaign, in a speech at the Reichstag, Hitler offered peace to France and Britain. There were only two issues to be resolved, he said: the boundaries of Poland and, more important, the restoration of European security. This required the nullification of Versailles, the return of the colonies, an international agreement on currencies in order to permit the expansion of international trade, and the reduction of armaments. This, he said, would be his last demand.

But the governments of France and Britain had reached a point of no return. Too many times had their hopes been betrayed and solemn promises been broken. Cut-throat competition strangling world trade had led to a war of words, an economic, monetary and tariff war, harbinger of an inescapable holocaust.

Across the Atlantic, America, secure and maintaining faith in its own destiny despite the hardships suffered by millions of unemployed, watched from a distance the Europeans readying themselves to tear each other to pieces for the second time in a generation.

7 Bretton Woods Revisited

> The idea may be good or bad, depending
> on the idea behind it.
> Harry Dexter White

The Bretton Woods Agreements, a 96-page document, were signed by the chairmen of 44 delegations on the evening of 22 July 1944, after more than three weeks of negotiations, following a memorable dinner; some delegates signed the next morning. They had acquiesced to endorse the Final Act drawn up by the American experts. The reader interested in the history of the negotiations preceding the signature, could consult my book *Bretton Woods: Birth of a Monetary System*.

On 17 July Keynes, whose time had been fully taken up by the Commission on the Bank, asked Morgenthau when he would be able to see the text of the agreement on the Fund: 'There are, you see, certain final technical matters we haven't considered at all, what the lawyers call the final act, which embodies the results of this Conference. No attempt has yet been made to draft that and it hasn't been considered by anybody. It is a matter all Delegations will want to have at least half a day to look at. At present, no one has seen, as a continuous narrative, the work which has been done, and I think it is not quite fair to the Delegations that they should be expected to pass so quickly on things they have never had a chance, really, of reading as a consecutive narrative. That is my feeling.'

'Thank you,' said Morgenthau.[1]

Two days later Morgenthau hurriedly called a seemingly unimportant meeting of the Steering Committee in charge of procedures. The chairmen of ten delegations were present, including the French and Belgian Finance Ministers Mendès-France and Gutt. Harry White was not there but had delegated his assistant Frank Coe. 'I think we will start and maybe Lord Keynes can catch up,' said Morgenthau.

Coe then explained that a document called the Final Act would put on record the agreements reached during the Conference. A group of experts would compile and commit to writing the decisions made by the various commissions. The commissions had worked so thoroughly and carefully that a meeting of the Coordinating Committee would be unnecessary. He therefore suggested that Mr Morgenthau, as Chairman of the Conference, be allowed to constitute the committee in charge of compilation and drafting of the Final Act of the Articles of Agreement.

'Would it be agreeable for you, gentlemen, to give me such authority?' Morgenthau asked. There was unanimous agreement.

Coe then read a resolution to the effect that 'the Government of the United States of America be authorized to publish the Final Act of this Conference. . . .'

'Any discussion?' Morgenthau asked. 'Would somebody move that we pass this resolution? All those in favor say aye. Contrary?' The resolution was approved.

Coe then explained that the Secretariat would write up the Final Act and that no changes could be made at the Closing Plenary Session. 'The signature, therefore, of the Final Act would be essentially, or entirely, a statement by the signer that he had attended the Conference and had witnessed these things being done.' The drafting would require a considerable amount of time and work and the Final Act would not be available for examination.

'What is your pleasure, gentlemen? You have heard this resolution. Would anybody move its adoption? Those in favor say aye. Contrary? If there is no other business, we could make this a record meeting,' Morgenthau concluded.[2]

It was also the most important meeting of the Conference, one that had been carefully planned. Harry White and his assistants were now free to write the Articles of Agreement exactly as they wanted, without any interference from Keynes, who would simply be asked to sign, like the chairmen of all the other delegations. The Final Act would be the charter, the Constitution. White's overwhelming concern was to put the dollar, next to gold, at the centre of the system. He had once briefly brought up the subject with Keynes, who flatly refused. It was never discussed again.

White would later jokingly tell Congressmen: 'We ended up by getting gold as the unit and calling it dollars.'[3]

Shortly after his return to London, Keynes became involved in a public controversy with several economists and politicians over the Articles of Agreement and was accused of having acquiesced to terms unacceptable to Great Britain. Clearly exasperated, he wrote White a long letter asking him to make some changes in the text. White did not answer. Keynes then strongly recommended that the government refuse to subscribe to a document which he had signed without reading:

That we did not openly and fully thrash out this issue was, of course, the initial mistake. As we all know, both the reason and the excuse for this is simply that we were not given time to do so. I myself had never seen the final text of the clauses now under discussion at the time when I signed the paper, since they had not emerged from the drafting committee soon enough for a complete text to be circulated.[4]

We, all of us, had to sign, of course, before we had had a chance of reading through a clean and consecutive copy of the document. All we had seen of it was the dotted line. Our only excuse is the knowledge that our hosts had made final arrangements to throw us out of the hotel, unhoused, disappointed, unaneled, within a few hours.[5]

Like most international conferences, Bretton Woods had witnessed a surfeit of rhetoric at the opening and closing sessions. The master of ceremonies was Morgenthau; Harry White's intellectual dominance and forceful personality pervaded the Conference; with his group of economists and lawyers he constituted the nerve centre and the powerhouse. Keynes was the opponent to be neutralized by relegating him and keeping him busy in Commission II. The other 700 delegates, very few of them familiar with the technicalities of international finance, were kept busy and entertained but had absolutely no influence on the outcome.

White very cleverly preserved the fictitious legal principle of equality between nations and the semblance of open discussion between equal delegations; he knew that long after the agitation and the noises of the Conference had died away, the only remaining document would be the Final Act; and this was under his exclusive control. He was eager to give the participants the impression that they were important and had something to contribute: 'They will make strong arguments . . . and if you can give them a little something, they feel that they have negotiated . . . and I think they feel better.' His assistant Dr Goldenweiser opined: 'Just make one general rule, that anybody can talk as long as he pleases provided he doesn't say anything! Separate the business of the Committee from the talk.'[6]

Dr E. A. Goldenweiser, Director of Research and Statistics of the Federal Reserve Board, recalled:

It was very hard work. The delegates of each country usually met by themselves in the morning. There were always two or three meetings of committees and commissions and sub- committees, and later there would be the big task of having all that combined, written and distributed by the next morning. There was a large force of stenographers and multigraphers who worked day and night. . . .

It was a combination of settling various conflicting interests, and at the same time hammering out specific provisions. They are inevitably complex because of the subject, and they are written in a legal language, which I have always found it difficult to understand. . . .

There were a great many varieties of people and a great many varieties of unintelligible English spoken. Most everything was said in what was supposed to be English. The Russians didn't speak English; neither did their interpreters. The French spoke English but always had trouble in being satisfied that their exact meaning was properly translated by their interpreters. . . . The Russians were an interesting group. I could not help feeling that they were struggling between the firing squad on the one hand and the English language on the other. They seemed to be very much afraid of the reactions in their own country, and didn't dare make a step without consultation by 'phone or cable with their Government.[7]

The war had mobilized the latent resources of American industrial capacity. The United States had become the leader and the fortress of the free world. Bretton Woods reflected this absolute political, industrial and financial supremacy.

WALL STREET BANKERS VS UNITED STATES TREASURY

To Secretary Morgenthau the establishment of the International Monetary Fund was the victorious consummation of his years of struggle to put the financial relations between nations exclusively in the hands of governments. The new organization would be an agent between sovereign nations granting financial help when and where needed and justified. The purpose was not profit but the promotion of international cooperation. During all his years as Secretary of the Treasury, Morgenthau's relations with the Wall Street bankers had been strained. He was convinced that the government had an important responsibility in the management of the economy. The manner in which the banking community had handled national and international affairs during the inter-war period had completely discredited private finance. High employment, stable prices and general welfare could only be achieved through government control of financial and monetary policy.

Morgenthau's primary objective as Secretary of the Treasury had been, he said, 'to move the financial center of the world from London and Wall

Street to the United States Treasury and to create a new concept between nations in international finance'.[8]

He wished to establish new institutions, 'instrumentalities of sovereign governments and not of private financial interests', and 'to drive . . . the usurious money lenders from the temple of international finance'. 'They were selfish,' he said, 'they put themselves above the interests of the people and the interests of the country. . . . The only flag they followed was their own gain. . . . The important issue was who governs, and the New Deal made the government govern American banking and monetary affairs, and I'm proud of my part in bringing that about.'[9]

He knew that the conservative business circles were successfully spreading the idea that business was winning the war by producing the tools despite the ineffectual harassments of the bureaucracy. He also knew the New Deal was in decline. During the Depression the bankers had gone into eclipse, their reputation badly damaged by Congressional investigations. The son of the great J. P. Morgan had been ridiculed when the papers published his picture with a midget put on his knee.

Loans available at low rates were not needed in times of depression. Now the war had brought back prosperity and the vast expansion of productive capacity had created the need for substantial credits. The large New York banks wanted to take advantage of the position of power the war had given them. They intended to resume their role as arbiters and providers of national and international loans and as intermediaries in international transactions. The City would play the role of a junior partner.

The Wall Street bankers had not been invited to participate in the Bretton Woods negotiations and they resented it as an encroachment by the government upon their legitimate domain. For more than a decade, ever since President Roosevelt entered the White House, they had been excluded from the country's financial policy-making.

Shortly after the publication of the Keynes and White plans, Randolph Burgess, vice-chairman of National City Bank, sent Morgenthau a confidential letter prepared by the Economic Policy Commission of the American Bankers Association. Knowing that Morgenthau had the power in his hands, he avoided offering criticism and a frontal attack. The problems to be faced after the war, he said, would be similar to those encountered after World War I, 'changed in form but in essence the same old problems of nations getting along together. The fashions in thinking about them change more than the problems themselves.' Monetary stability would be the first requirement:

Ranking close to the hazard of war as an obstacle to human material progress is the changing value of money. The interchange of goods between people that constitutes trade is normally carried on with money. When there is question about the value of money trade is disorganized, dormant, or hectic. . . . Especially is the advance planning on which full employment so largely depends blocked by the doubt of money.[10]

The stabilization of currencies in recent years had depended largely upon the relation of the pound to the dollar, the Sterling block and the Dollar block. If this relation could be fixed, much more than half the job would be done. Since the stabilization of the dollar in 1934, the American currency had been the pivot of the world financial system. The United States should take the leadership in bringing about general currency stability and it was doubtful whether this could be achieved through an international institution made up mainly of debtor countries.

The New York bankers were in a position to cause considerable trouble. Their reports and their public speeches were usually well prepared and received considerable press coverage. They blamed the government for having rejected the Peace Treaty, and for having declined to participate in the League of Nations, the World Court and the Bank for International Settlements. They were also critical of Roosevelt's decision to torpedo the London Economic Conference in 1933. The bankers had no doubt that Congress would kill the plan and that they need not exert themselves too much. The leading bankers, however, kept feeding articles to the press. Leon Fraser, President of the First National Bank of New York, explained:

Despite its pretentious ring, international money is not difficult to define or understand. It is money that will be accepted internationally as a satisfactory means of payment in transactions between people in different nations. It must be the pivot to which the currencies of the principal trading nations are attached. . . . As the international money of tomorrow I propose a dollar-sterling standard to which the nations shall be invited to repair.[11]

The President of W. R. Grace & Co. expressed a similar view: 'The world believes in the dollar . . . not only a great opportunity but a very serious duty lies before the American banker. His task is to assume world leadership in accordance with a plan which he should work out with our Government and with the Federal Reserve Bank. . . . The Keynes Plan is very clever, a scheme for trading in what are virtually "chips".'[12]

A few days after the publication of the postwar currency plans, the *Völkischer Beobachter* had observed that trade between Germany and other countries was not transacted by means of currencies that were completely foreign to it.

> Because we refused to use the pound and the dollar in our clearing system, the British and particularly the Americans were mad at us. We only wanted to exchange goods needed on both sides. According to the old rules of the game, every national economy depended for its foreign trade on international finance. . . .
>
> The German clearing system is the most modern mechanism for the international exchange of goods and services. . . . When we organized our clearing system we did not start with international conferences; we started with the exchange of goods. . . . In Germany we have created employment not because we developed a monetary theory but because we started working.[13]

The controversy between the Wall Street bankers and the Treasury, while it appeared to be over technicalities, involved in fact a more fundamental issue: would the power centre of international finance rest with the private banks or with the governments?

As the Bretton Woods Conference started, the barrage of criticism and opposition by the bankers became more articulate and virulent. They had a big stake in international finance. They feared that the Bretton Woods proposals would bring their international operations too much under control of governments, just as the banking, stock exchange and other New Deal regulatory measures had curbed the control they once exercised over national finance. They followed the proceedings closely and, while they were excluded from the Conference, they redoubled their campaign with the help of prominent economists. A few observers understood what was really at issue:

> I suppose at the heart of the matter is the fact that this machinery would be put in the hands of public servants, paid executives of the governments involved, rather than in the group of private and powerful international bankers in 'the City' in London, and in lower Manhattan in New York. You can see at once why there is a row involved. . . . [It was] one of those battles among the financially and intellectually mighty in which the merits of the contending positions usually remain for the most part obscure to the vast audience.[14]

The bankers who campaigned against the Fund spoke with the authority of experts who had a long experience in international finance and whose views commanded attention. Since they intended to accomplish the same results as the Treasury, but by different methods, the question was whether the governments or the private bankers should be in charge of international finance.

The *Milwaukee Journal* seems to have expressed the majority opinion: 'In view of the billions of dollars unwisely lent abroad by bankers in the twenties, and subsequently lost by American investors, it does not seem reasonable that the objections of these gentlemen should be given great weight.'[15]

On 4 January 1945 Morgenthau and his staff met with several bankers representing the various banking associations. He asked Burgess, who had requested the meeting, how he wished to proceed. Burgess read a report recommending that the Fund be disregarded because it would grant credit to countries that were not necessarily creditworthy, simply because they had an absolute right to draw.

Morgenthau, speaking from a position of power, stated that the bankers had the right to make whatever technical suggestions they wanted, but that in the end they should approve of the Agreements as an essential instrument for international financial cooperation.

Burgess answered that 'if it were this or nothing, he would take this'. The Secretary said 'it was this or nothing, and the bankers ought to recognize this in their report'. He thanked them for coming to the Treasury.[16]

The banker's report finally recommended that the International Bank for Reconstruction and Development be created, and that certain elements of the Fund be incorporated in the Bank. The Fund was too big, too elaborate, too complicated, too difficult for the public to understand. The language of the agreement was so vague as to be susceptible to widely differing interpretations and did not stipulate that the loans should be good loans. The *New York Times* hailed the bankers' report as 'constructive and statesmanlike'.[17]

Morgenthau was furious. He discussed the report with his staff. 'We might distort it,' White suggested, 'and say the speculators are against it.' After a long discussion, Morgenthau decided he would meet the press: 'It is up to the Government to take the risk on the interest rates and not up to the individuals. . . . Sure we are taking the risk. It is better for us to take the risk and spread it among forty-four partners than to have five banks in New York dictate foreign exchange rates, with the five banks in line, and having London lead us around by the nose, which they have done in the last one hundred years.'

White agreed: 'This is a fight between international bankers and Government . . . the fight has begun. . . . They left us no alternative.'[18]

For several weeks the public debate over Bretton Woods made headline news; several groups bought space in the papers to advocate the plans, others recommended rejection of the Fund.

By the end of May 1945 the British Embassy advised London that all organized resistance against Bretton Woods had collapsed and that the enactment by Congress seemed assured.

CONGRESS DEBATES

President Roosevelt had forwarded the Articles of Agreement to Congress with an appeal for speedy approval. The Treasury had organized a nationwide campaign with little result. Confronted with 'the most intricate economic document that has ever come before Congress in the history of the country', both Houses probed the advantages and the risks. It was generally admitted that the wording was 'so involved, so ambiguous, so evasive, so full of provisions and exceptions at cross-purposes to each other that they defy understanding'.

Opponents described the agreements as: 'a scheme to get American money under false pretenses'; 'the most colossal monetary and financial swindle ever attempted'; 'a trick to sell America to the lowest bidder for worthless foreign currency'. Senator Taft said it was 'like pouring money down a rathole'.[19]

As usual Taft dominated the Senate debate: 'Undoubtedly, it is a technical subject. . . . The truth is there are very few experts on this subject. Most of those who are quoted here have no more brains and no more knowledge than the average Senator.'

The opposition, however vocal, was limited: mid-western isolationists were hostile to the idea that an international organization would have jurisdiction over the domestic policies of the United States. The campaign by the New York banks had convinced several members of Congress. Others remembered the depression, for which the bankers were blamed, and the billions of dollars of worthless German bonds; they had become exasperated by the bankers' campaign. 'Perhaps I should not mention bankers, because it is a bad word around here,' said Representative Buffett.

Representative Patman, a long-time critic of the international bankers, said:

There is an international banking ring with headquarters in this country that is opposing this legislation with all their power and might. In every way possible they are opposing it. It is against their selfish greedy interest for this bill to become a law. They do not want these agreements. They are the vultures that sit around waiting for some country to get into trouble so that they can help bail it out at a big price and to the disadvantage of the other countries. . . . It is the international bankers, the clique – not all of them, but those who are profiting most by chaos in the world – who are opposing this legislation.[20]

Mr. Fraser was a great international banker . . . as a symbol he represented, I guess, the biggest bank of its kind in the entire world. I do not believe that bank had anything in common with the ordinary banks of our country. It was a bank that had only 1200 customers. No person could maintain a deposit in the bank less than $1 000 000. . . . If you had $500 000, the teller at the bank window would convince you that they could not render you the service that you were entitled to receive from that bank, and that you should go to another institution.[21]

Representative Flood recalled the problems caused by currency speculation:

With world money markets and standards the subject of economic warfare, anyone trading in the world market never could tell, from one moment to the next, where his business was. The only profits made in this type of international piracy were made by the small handful of economic freebooters who unscrupulously manipulated the rates of exchange, sending the value of all moneys affected up and down in a sea of chaos and money madness. Is it any wonder war followed? Small wonder, indeed.[22]

The overwhelming majority was in favour of Bretton Woods:

It is significant that the Independent Bankers Association has endorsed the entire Bretton Woods proposal. But the opposition of the great international bankers to Bretton Woods has stemmed from the fact that they see in it a proposal which for the first time in all history would take from them the opportunity to manipulate international monetary movements for private gain and without reference to the effect of such movements upon the economic well-being of millions of people within the nations of the world.[23]

Bretton Woods . . . recognizes that international exchange rates should be adjusted in orderly fashion for domestic needs and domestic policies that will promote full employment.[24]

Senator Bushfield thought there was little difference between money given away by the American public and money given away by the government:

> It is very clear in my mind that following the last World War we loaned $11 000 000 000 to foreign nations, and very little of it has ever been repaid. In addition, about $14 000 000 000 worth of foreign bonds were peddled among the people of this country by a few international bankers, and very few of these bonds have been repaid. As a matter of fact, a definite fraud was perpetrated upon the people of this country at that time, and it took in all classes of our people. Now, under the Bretton Woods Agreements, we are proposing to loan or give away – whichever it might be called – more billions of dollars, and I am wondering what the distinction is between the fraud which was perpetrated 25 years ago and the present proposal.[25]

The House approved the Bretton Woods Bill by 345 votes to 18; the Senate by 61 to 16. In London Keynes had recommended that the government reject the Agreements because they were 'either self-contradictory or hopelessly obscure'. But the United States had made ratification a condition for the execution of a financial agreement signed in Washington and providing a $3.75 billion loan for Britain. Russia never ratified the Agreements. Most other countries applied for membership. The International Monetary Fund was to promote consultation and co-operation on international monetary problems.

8 The Americanization of Europe

American companies have been established in Europe since the late 1800s. Many more set up shop during the booming 1920s. But after World War II the influx became massive. Two accidents of history had destroyed the accumulated wealth and wrecked the economic, financial and political power of Europe.

The war, rather than the New Deal, had ended the Great Depression. The United States had emerged from the war with its industry intact, its economy operating at high levels and an unquestioned economic, financial, military and technological supremacy. Americans came to be lulled into a frame of mind which convinced them that this state of affairs was a natural consequence of innate American superiority in production, politics and economic management.

Europe, with its backward economy, was a market wide open for the sophisticated products of United States companies, manufacturing and selling almost everything, from soup to computers, from thermostats to toothpaste, from dog food to mining machinery.

Some countries welcomed and attracted these investments; elsewhere they were less desirable. An evaluation of the advantages and disadvantages, past, present and future of these investments is beyond the scope of this book.

American companies had a choice between starting a fresh with a wholly-owned subsidiary, a joint venture with an established company or the acquisition of a going concern. Many family-held factories in the hands of third generation business-bored heirs, tired of competition, were available at very attractive prices.

At the end of the war the United States held 60 per cent of the world's gold reserves and in 1947 its trade surplus was $10.1 billion. It seemed there would be for many years an acute dollar shortage. Ten years later the IMF began to call the United States' balance of payments deficit 'a problem'. In 1970 the deficit reached $10.7 billion and the following year the United States ran its first trade deficit since 1893; it amounted to $2.5 billion.

United States exports had traditionally exceeded by far its imports, but American companies escalated their stampede to set up production and distribution facilities in Europe. Between 1950 and 1963 United

71

States investments jumped from $2 billion to over $8 billion. When a company in one branch of industry made the move, its competitors felt they had to follow, lest they be left behind in the race. Over 300 American companies settled in Belgium, over 250 chose Holland and possibly 600 set up operations in France. In the early 1960s about 3000 American companies maintained European manufacturing activities of one type or another.[1]

From the very beginning, most of these investments were profitable. In 1970 the book value of United States foreign investment exceeded $80 billion and earned around $11 billion.[2]

In 1955 six American banks had branches in London. By 1970 their number had increased to 34. The Bank of England welcomed these new-comers, provided they had a substantial domestic balance sheet and a good reputation. They needed no capital. They simply opened an office, borrowed dollars from their head office or Eurodollars in the interbank market and started lending. Since Eurodollars could not be used as law-ful money in any country, the borrowers had to exchange them against local currencies. The Eurodollars for which the economy had no use sim-ply stayed in the Eurobanking system, available for speculation.

The European governments were now confronted with an entirely new problem. From 1958 to 1969 the Community of the Six had achieved complete tariff union and thus created a free trade zone. It had estab-lished the common agricultural policy. Logically, in a world where tariff barriers were progressively coming down, it would have to free capital movements within its borders. About 60 per cent of European interna-tional trade was conducted within the Community. When the decision was made to take this decisive step, it applied not only to the national currencies of the member countries but also to the stateless dollar. The fact that Eurodollars were considered by the United States government as international private money does not seem to have been clearly per-ceived by the European authorities.

On the eve of his retirement, in December 1969, Bundesbank president Karl Blessing expressed concern over the fact that the United States accumulated vast amounts of dollars in European central banks: 'But naturally this cannot go on *ad infinitum*, because the liabilities of American banks (which is to say the American economy) have already risen to some $28 billion, just to banks in the rest of the world.' He thought 'the Euromarket was created, of course, by the American pay-ments deficit.'[3]

Several central banks converted dollars into gold, a move initially wel-comed by the United States government. But when it became evident that the volume of dollars held abroad far exceeded United States gold reserves, a considerable debate arose concerning a possible devaluation of the dollar. In mid-1962, the United States owned $13 billion in gold reserves against outstanding foreign claims of $68 billion, of which $50 billion were held by foreign central banks.

Senator John F. Kennedy, convinced that in the long run, a country, big or small, just like an individual or a company, could not spend more than it earned – with borrowings to bridge the gaps – had promised that, if elected, he would defend the value of the dollar and its soundness. After his election he used to tell his advisers 'that the two things that scared him most were nuclear war and the payments deficit'.[4]

But his Secretary of the Treasury, banker Douglas Dillon, told him 'the United States should continue as banker of the world'. President Kennedy was soon convinced that United States deficits were 'a needed source of growth of world reserves'. The balance of payments problem suddenly disappeared. It had been treated for years as a major problem, plunging the Administration into despair; suddenly the Department of Commerce announced it as a 'non-event'. Reference was made to the 'roundabout' flows of dollars between Europe and the United States. The world was on a dollar standard. The thought relieved the Americans of the anxiety that had prevailed for so long, while the balance of payments problem 'settled into the quintessence of innocuous desuetude', as the *Journal of Commerce* noted.

When European governments criticized the way the United States handled its balance of payments, American officials criticized European failure to develop adequate capital markets. When the Europeans criticized the Americans for creating inflation in Europe, the Americans confused them, stating that they were relying too heavily on monetary policy and not enough on fiscal policy to restrain aggregate demand.[5]

President de Gaulle undertook a solitary fight to contain the American hegemony; incensed by the fact that foreign corporations were acquiring control of vital French industries and paying with worthless IOUs, which they freely exchanged for European currencies, he tried in vain to persuade the other Common Market governments to restrain American investment, which he considered 'a kind of expropriation'. His financial adviser, Jacques Rueff, denounced the American privilege to abuse 'the wonderful secret of a tearless deficit which permits giving without taking, lending without borrowing and acquiring without paying'. He also saw in 'the blind, absurd and monstrous proliferation of the Eurodollar the utmost threat to the stability of the western world'. The claim that the deficit, the 'swaps', Roosa bonds and other gimmicks were a source of reserve growth needed for the common benefit was a 'scandalous hypocritical fraud'.[6]

The French protests found no echo across the Rhine. Germany, the powerhouse of Europe, constantly trying, since the defeat of Nazism, to regain at any price its place among civilized nations, was inhibited by the politico-military vicissitudes of history and depended for its security on the presence of American troops.

De Gaulle was also very much aware of the special relationship between Britain and the United States. He considered Britain a vassal to America, ready to follow Washington's instructions in exchange for financial benefits: Britain, he said, was paying lip service to the European Community but was in fact America's Trojan horse. On 14 January 1963 he announced the French veto to British membership in the Common Market. If Britain were admitted, 'in the end there would appear a colossal Atlantic Community under American dependence and leadership which would soon completely swallow up the economy of the European Community'. To many Americans the French attitude was incomprehensible; how could France, after having been saved twice, be so ungrateful?

Some American economists, led by Milton Friedman, constantly stated that the dollar problem was indeed a European problem, of no concern to the United States. In September 1970 the *Süddeutsche Zeitung* interviewed Friedman: 'You are chained to the dollar like a prisoner,' Nixon's adviser and chief ideologist said. 'If the Federal Republic wants to recover an autonomous control over its monetary policy, it has to put an end to the fixed-exchange-rate system and introduce floating rates.'[7]

The vice-president of the Bundesbank, Otmar Emminger, expressed concern in February 1969 about another aspect of the problem: a system in which one currency has a special role as a reserve currency can function only as long as this currency remains stable. If inflation in the United States continued at current levels of 4 to 5 per cent as it was in 1968 – intolerable by German standards – the system would break down.

By 1970 the German inflation rate had doubled. The dollars injected into the European economy rendered the central banks helpless. According to classic textbook recipes, putting the economy through a squeeze of tight money and tight budgets, resulting in a rise of unemployment, was bound to slow down activity and inflationary pressure. Now the classic relation between unemployment and wages completely failed to operate. It became apparent that Eurodollars flooding through the banking system, spreading disorder, instability and occasionally chaos, were the principal culprits of the inflationary tide. On several occasions a monetary squeeze in Germany caused a large inflow of foreign funds into the country. When these currencies were presented to the Bundesbank in exchange for marks, the domestic money supply increased.

While American companies and large corporations were treated to prodigious international capital markets and a glittering array of financial services and products, smaller entrepreneurs had to be satisfied with sparsely granted bank loans and credits. In Europe and in the United States, governments, faced with the insoluble dilemma of stagflation, tried to slow down wage increases. They discovered that without the cooperation of organized labour they would fail. And organized labour simply refused cooperation. Inflationary expectations had infiltrated mass psychology, pushing trade unions to demand wage increases far outstripping productivity, thus fuelling the inflationary spiral.

The European governments now awoke to the belated realization of the extent to which the Eurodollar market artfully circumvented their laws, regulations and policies. Europe had failed to provide a united front and the necessary awareness, understanding and leadership to counter the recurrent speculative assaults.

In Switzerland, Germany and a few other countries, a desire for stability permeates the collective psychology of the population. Convinced that 'inflation, like dictatorship, can only be curbed before it takes over', and that 'inflation is a fraud committed against the people', there exists a consensus to restrain inflation fever.

The French, the Italians, the British and a few others had been conditioned for years to a 'normal' dose of inflation, considered by politicians as an elixir of the economy and a stimulant to employment. In Britain inflation had increased to about 9 per cent in 1970, but the British government had witnessed with great satisfaction how the dollar had resuscitated the City as the world's financial centre. The former Chancellor of the Exchequer R. Maudling had once described the United States' deficit problem as 'less one of a balance of payments than a balance of generosity'.[8]

When the French Finance Minister, Giscard d'Estaing, criticized the creation of deficits by the Americans, the answer was that 'the reserve currency status had been thrust upon the US dollar, not deliberately sought'. Those who complained about investment by United States corporations would probably complain just as loudly if the United States' payments deficit did not exist.

Since 1964 controversy about the international monetary system had been out in the open. The Committee of Twenty was one of the numerous study groups involved in discussions about monetary problems. Article VIII of the Bretton Woods Agreements provided that member countries could impose controls on international capital transactions but not on current transactions. When the subject was discussed, American negotiators considered the distinction irrational: the United States was exporting capital to invest in Europe, thus stimulating the economy.

To most officials economic efficiency arguments for freer trade in goods logically carried over to freer trade in money. But to many European officials the purpose of international economic relations was trade in goods, and since capital flows could affect the exchange rate at which goods traded, those flows should be controlled. European attitudes favoring control of capital flows were a mental carryover from the Bretton Woods system where short-term capital flows tended to be regarded as 'disequilibrating'.[9]

In 1964 Britain had a considerable balance of payments deficit; the government imposed a 15 per cent surcharge on imports and granted a tax rebate on exports. Speculators, foreseeing a devaluation of the pound, jumped at the opportunity and started selling sterling short. The Chancellor of the Exchequer blamed the 'gnomes of Zurich' whereas the centre of the speculation was right in his own backyard. When another crisis erupted in 1966 the government started thinking about letting the pound float.

The period 1965–71 was one of intense monetary turmoil. Monetary and financial news became headline material. Since the early 1960s, when the Eurodollar market came out in the open, it had exploded by leaps and bounds, outside any government control, and far beyond the needs of industry and commerce. These stateless dollars could only be used for speculation.

THE GREAT GOLD RUSH OF 1967–8

In 1934 the Gold Reserve Act set the price of gold at $35 an ounce. In the late 1950s, when the American balance of payments started moving into deficit, it seemed the dollar might have to be devalued. In 1960 gold briefly reached $40 before receding; speculation intensified when it became evident that the imbalance between the United States' payments deficit and the gold reserves would compel the government to raise the price or suspend sales.

In 1961 the United States and Britain decided to set up the Gold Pool; six other countries soon joined. Rueff's repeated calls for an increase of the gold price and de Gaulle's press conference of 4 February 1965, when he recommended substituting gold for the dollar as the basis of the monetary system – 'gold, which does not change in nature, which can be shaped either into bars, ingots or coins, which has no nationality, which is considered, in all places and at all times, the immutable and fiduciary value par excellence' – had persuaded many people in France and elsewhere that the price of gold was due to increase considerably.

General de Gaulle had also replenished the vaults of the Banque de France; when he came to power, France was saddled with an enormous debt and had practically exhausted its gold reserves. Ten years later the French central bank had the third largest reserve in the Western world. The press campaigns sponsored by South Africa induced many private buyers to invest in gold.

Washington sent out veiled threats from time to time hinting that it might refuse to sell gold if withdrawals continued; there was reluctance, however, to counter the speculation, since this could have been interpreted as an admission that the dollar was no longer 'as good as gold'. As the price continued to rise and speculators bought increasing quantities of the metal from the central banks, the Gold Pool was closed. No more gold would be sold to the public nor to central banks continuing to satisfy the demand of private buyers. This break with tradition symbolized the fact that gold was no longer an indispensable element in the international monetary system. Understandably, the decision was denounced by General de Gaulle.[10]

DOLLAR IMPERIALISM

The continuing payments deficits of the United States increased doubts about the ability of governments to keep the Bretton Woods monetary system functioning. In May 1968 the French penchant for occasional anarchy led to violent demonstrations in Paris followed by a general strike throughout the country. The costs were enormous. Prime Minister Pompidou had to grant substantial wage increases resulting in an immediate rise in consumer spending and prices. Imports suddenly swelled, the balance of payments deteriorated, forcing the government to introduce import quotas and to sell part of its gold reserves. The impression grew that the franc would have to be devalued.

German prices meanwhile had remained stable and year after year the country accumulated a growing export surplus. According to the IMF rules the franc seemed overvalued and the mark undervalued. Speculators holding Eurodollars started buying marks. In the first three weeks of November 1968 the Bundesbank was forced to buy about $2.5 billion. In one day it took $800 million.

The German government, still refusing to revalue, put a tax on exports and a tax remission on imports. The British, the French and the Americans demanded a revaluation, but the Germans refused, arguing that their economy was sound and that it was up to the other countries to take remedial action. Also, the Common Market uniform agricultural prices, negotiated after years of haggling, would have meant lower prices for the German farmers.

Early in 1969 de Gaulle organized a referendum; he was defeated. His abrupt resignation on 28 April 1969 marked the beginning of a rush into D-marks. The same day, the German Finance Minister Strauss suggested publicly that Germany might revalue the mark.

Starting at the end of April, a torrent of dollars poured into the Bundesbank. On 9 May it had to take in more than $1.3 billion. The German government coalition was split: the Social Democrats advocated revaluation; Strauss and the Christian Democrats opposed it. On 9 May the German cabinet rejected revaluation 'for eternity', and introduced new controls on the dollar inflow, which would prove ineffective. On 8 August the franc was devalued, and on 29 September Germany let the D-mark float. On 24 October, after the elections, the mark was revalued by 9.3 per cent. The first major currency crisis in Europe after the devaluation of the pound in 1967, came to an end.

It had provoked a grave deterioration of political and economic relations between the major European countries; it had caused angry outbursts in an atmosphere of mistrust and animosity. It had forced the Bundesbank to buy billions of unwanted dollars and it had liquidated French reserves. The turmoil left scars in the European landscape. Those who built up the crisis and who finally triggered it, the speculators, securely counted the chips, ready for the next round.

From there on monetary upheavals became a recurrent phenomenon; each successive crisis inexorably created the psychological basis for the next, as progressively more banks and more of their clients participated in the action. The Pavlovian reaction of governments, when their central bank came under attack, invariably produced the same ritual: resolute statements about the solidity of their currency and about their determination to defend it; very soon, after their central bank had been overrun, forced to concede that their parities, after all, were not as solid as they had claimed, they graced their surrender with euphemisms and bureaucratic prose. After each convulsion, the old game started all over again and after each coup the speculators pocketed the profits.

Central bank reserves were an inadequate counterweight to such destabilizing forces. If the Bundesbank stood ready to absorb $3 billion in defence of the fixed D-mark rate, it would automatically get that amount; if it is was ready to take double, it would get double.

In November 1968 the Group of Ten had staged a simulacrum of investigation on how to dry up this 'hot money sponge', but since the Americans and British were part of the Group the outcome was obvious. There was no formula anyway to 'recycle' the Eurodollars to their creators. Eminent economists began to argue that the causes of the monetary disturbances lay with the economic policies of the governments and with the rigidities of the IMF rules. The lessons of the thirties seemed completely forgotten. The Europeans were divided among themselves. De Gaulle tried without success to oppose American hegemony; but the 'events' of May 1968 moderated French aspirations to leadership. The Germans were anxious to be accepted as a civilized nation, avoiding anything that could be interpreted as if they were again throwing their weight around. The Eurodollar had made London the world's financial centre: the government was not going to kill the goose. The other countries were reduced to making proposals and taking sides, hoping to influence the innumerable meetings of ministers, central bankers, committees and study groups; their impact remained secondary.

Washington had come to consider axiomatic that what was good for the United States dollar was good for everybody else, since the world was dependent upon the dollar as the international standard. Many years of undisputed hegemony had accustomed the Americans to think that their views represented the general interest; they expressed impatience and annoyance at anybody obstructing their plans. The fact that they had for years financed the defence of the free world and maintained the 'Pax Americana' entitled them to special gratitude, which included the unlimited accumulation of dollars.

THE GENTLEMAN FROM TEXAS

In 1971 the United States was experiencing a sort of economic menopause; no innovative response could be found to stave off the rising tide of Toyotas, Volkswagens and other imports inundating the market. The most dynamic export industry seemed to be soy beans. Nixon was looking for a way to break the American economy out of stagflation.

The United States' balance of payments was in trouble for reasons which did not command sympathy in other countries: the Vietnam war, excessive foreign investment and tourism. The size of what was considered the dollar overhang swelled year after year and by 1971 over $50 billion were reluctantly held by European central banks. In 1971 a number of small countries began to draw gold from the Federal Reserve. President Nixon panicked: it would be preferable to face a dollar crisis a year before the election than in the course of the campaign. A number of prominent academic economists blamed the United States payments deficit on the Bretton Woods fixed exchange-rate system. President Nixon decided their analysis was correct and resolved to act on it.

The vast and complex international consultative machinery could not possibly provide an answer and was to be discarded. The United States would take care of itself, all by itself. It was a tremendous challenge requiring an exceptional man. The President decided to let his Secretary of the Treasury take the situation in hand. Connally was indeed an exception at the head of the United States Treasury, in more than one way. He was neither a banker nor an academic. The President had been impressed with his toughness and decisiveness as the Democrat governor of the Lone Star state.

Tall, handsome, superbly tailored, a flamboyant and self-confident big-business lawyer used to frontal attacks and subtle bluffing, a master of urbane ruthlessness, Connally could be as suave as any blue-blooded sophisticate. He became the epitome of the towering and patronizing negotiators the United States government appointed in troubled times to deal with the Europeans.

Alternating well-worded, nicely polished phrases and dignified utterances evoking empathy, with outrageous demands and threats, convinced that attack is the best defence, his showdown tactics and his style of diplomatic bluster bullied his European 'friends and allies' on their currency parities, their trade practices, their defence and foreign policies. His performance dismayed his spectators with one notable exception: the German Finance and Economics Minister, Karl Schiller.

An economics professor, Schiller had joined the Social-Democrat party at a time when it was still very much 'socialist'. A free-market advocate, he represented the extreme conservative fraction of the party and was unpopular among labour unions and militants. Despite his controversial position, his career in politics had been surprisingly meteoric. He had developed a warm friendship with John Connally, calling him 'a full-blooded politician'. Connally returned the compliment: 'I am a Schiller fan.'[11]

Early in April 1971 over $1 billion had moved into Germany in a three-day span. On May 3 some $1.2 billion poured into the country; the following day, in the space of one hour, another $1 billion rushed in.

What galls bankers elsewhere in Europe is the conviction that it was Germany – or more precisely Karl Schiller, Germany's loquacious economics minister that really started money moving in the first place by openly flirting with the possibility of a realignment of currency values. Said a top official at one European central bank: 'We can't blame the U.S. for this. It's Schiller's fault, and it's up to the Germans to stop the crisis. Schiller really started the pot boiling last week by arguing with his Common Market partners that, since the U.S. was not going to oblige by devaluing the dollar, they should let їּ eir currencies float against the dollar. . . . By Wednesday morning it was a full-blown crisis – the 'Schiller crisis' as central bankers outside Germany called it.[12]

Nixon's negotiating position in international monetary affairs was obviously very weak; he realized that his only weapon was a unilateral United States *blitzkrieg* attack, hoping it would quickly overwhelm all organized resistance. Bluffing to disguise the weakness of the United States 'stance, offering a token concession and then demanding a *quid pro quo* for his munificence, Connally's policies, rhetoric and style were reminiscent of pre-war tactics, when every country attempted to save jobs by exporting unemployment, using economic muscle to enforce bargains. Early in May 1971 Schiller openly stated that since the United States was not going to devalue the dollar, European currencies should be revalued. The French vetoed the idea because it would have meant acceptance of a de facto dollar standard. The dispute triggered off a major monetary crisis. Once speculation started, it turned into a stampede. Speculators poured the – then unbelievable – amount of $1 billion into the German banking system in a single hour. Large amounts of dollars were also exchanged for Dutch guilders, Austrian schillings and Swiss francs. Overcome by the onslaught, the central banks decided to suspend all dealings in dollars. On 9 May, after a 20-hour session, the Common Market finance ministers agreed to Schiller's demand to let the D-mark float, despite the strain it would put on the agricultural policy and on the integration schedule.

The Americans felt that if their policies hurt European plans it was up to the Europeans to take appropriate measures to protect themselves; but conflicting interests, traditions and polities prevented the various governments from taking a coordinated stand and action.

During the second week of August 1971 Britain had asked to reactivate the Federal Reserve's swap lines to cover hundreds of millions of dollars they had been forced to absorb recently. Connally, misreading the request, told Nixon that the British wanted gold, perhaps as much as $3 billion, more than one-quarter of the remaining United States gold stock. As one close observer noted:

> All Connally wanted to hear was that some limey wanted gold and his mind was made up. What mattered to him was that the Europeans had betrayed the United States by refusing to accept the dollar as the universal currency and they had to be punished for it.[13]

After several months of debate within the Administration, where fundamental philosophies and attitudes had been challenged and the options for action studied, President Nixon had made up his mind. Rather than organizing an international conference, he decided to hit hard. Political prestige is deeply involved in international monetary affairs. Instead of letting it seem a defeat, Nixon wanted to present his decision as a political triumph.

On 15 August 1971, with a few sentences, he demolished the fulcrum of the world's monetary mechanism: 'In recent weeks, the speculators have been waging an all-out war on the American dollar. . . . Accordingly, I have directed the Secretary of the Treasury to take the action necessary to defend the dollar against the speculators. I have directed Secretary Connally to suspend temporarily the convertibility of the dollar into gold or other reserve assets.'

The rules laid down at Bretton Woods came to an end. In addition, Nixon imposed a temporary 10 per cent surcharge on most imports, a totally illegal measure under the GATT Agreement. Nixon's rhetoric about liberal trade contradicted his mercantilist policies aiming at curbing imports while pushing to expand American products and American foreign investment.

Moves that break the rules must be presented as 'temporary', a face-saving device that fooled no one. There was no consultation before the event, there was no promise of cooperation after. There was a threat of worse to come if the President did not get his way. Neither the IMF nor the Federal Reserve had been consulted. Connally had invited the managing director of the Fund, Mr Schweitzer, to his office to watch Nixon on television. The announcement was as brutal as the decision itself.

The notification of a 10 per cent surcharge on imports caused fear and resentment in the international export industry. Japan felt insulted by the decision: 30 per cent of its exports went to the United States. The United

States also absorbed about 10 per cent of German exports. Connally remarked: 'It really shook 'em up.'

Immediately after Nixon's announcement, the Common Market countries embarked upon a search for a joint position. Germany wanted the Community currencies to float together against the dollar, while France insisted on a two-tier exchange separating commercial operations from purely financial and speculative transactions. The French government issued a communiqué blaming Washington for the 'perturbations of the international monetary system'. Recent events were due to the American payments deficit and to the fact that the United States government had consistently refused to correct it. In fact, the mass of dollars flooding the European exchanges were simply Eurodollars which the United States government considered 'stateless'.

Karl Schiller resented the statement made by the French government and clashed with Giscard d'Estaing. 'The French government refuses to be lectured by you' said the French minister, accusing Schiller of conducting a satellite policy. Obviously, the disagreement on monetary policy was mainly based on the political relationship of the two countries with Washington.

Schiller repeatedly stated that it was important not to retaliate, not to engage in economic warfare, because this would incite the Americans to hit back even harder. The dollar had been at the centre of the par value of currencies established at Bretton Woods. The dollar was the unit of account, the currency of settlement, the intervention currency, the dominant trading currency and the major reserve asset.

The central banks were committed to buy with their own currencies any amount of dollars as soon as the United States currency touched its lower limit of 1 per cent. According to the rules, they could then exchange these dollars against gold. Thus the American banking community, led by the Administration, brought the gold-exchange standard to an end. Although the European governments did not immediately seem to realize it, they were on a dollar standard. It took them some time to discover that the United States was not playing by the rules of the game. Those who protested soon found out they could bark but not bite.

WE HAVE A GREAT DEAL OF CLOUT

Suddenly, overnight, the dollar was floating. To importers and exporters involved in trade with the United States, floating became a nightmare. For years they had known that the dollar was worth DM 4.2, BFr 50,

L 620; £1 was worth $2.40 since the 1967 devaluation. Currency parities were self-evident; contracts were securely signed, everyone knowing how much he would have to pay and how much he would receive. Very few had ever heard of Bretton Woods. Then the newspaper headlines announced that Bretton Woods was dead.

American importers were treated as swindlers and cheaters when they paid in devalued dollars, although they bore no responsibility for the parity changes. Business relationships involving mutual trust with European suppliers became at times very tense. Nobody seemed to understand who – or what – was behind the turmoil, until it gradually became clear that the culprits were those who manipulated currencies by making the unit of account the object of speculation.

Nixon's brutal cleverness had deeply shocked European public opinion. On 19 August the Common Market finance ministers had an emergency meeting in Brussels. Schiller wanted the Community currencies to float together against the dollar. France wanted a two-tier market. Anthony Barber, the British Chancellor of the Exchequer told reporters repeatedly: 'I have come to listen.' He 'seemed very candid and humorous'. The compromise formulas suggested by the Benelux countries were rejected. No agreement was reached.[14]

Europe was fundamentally divided. Once again, only France tried to oppose the Americans. The British government was mainly concerned with the City's interests. Bonn was torn between the constant fear of doing anything that might smack of anti-Americanism and the legitimate desire to protect its economy.

As billions of dollars continued to flood the German market, reluctantly accumulated by the Bundesbank, Schiller and Bundesbank president Klasen argued vehemently about the policy to adopt. Almost alone, against protests by German industry, Schiller wanted the mark to float while Klasen wanted to impose exchange controls. Fritz Berg, president of the Federation of German Industries, prophesied: 'Thousands of businesses are already bankrupt. Only they don't know it yet.' Floating was 'the greatest stupidity we have committed in the past 70 years'.[15] On several occasions Schiller was cornered and had to compromise. *Der Spiegel* observed that 'The Americans thought they were going to lose their most faithful financier in Europe.'[16]

Whereas the advent of floating caused disarray and embarrassment to commerce and industry, the Anglo-Saxon banking community jubilated. As mouthpiece for the City, *The Economist* was delighted: 'Floating can be fun. . . . All has been splendidly calm in the great float. The politicians should stay away on their holidays, and let the foreign exchange dealers handle matters.'[17]

Companies involved in international trade saw it differently:

> Nobody knows exactly where the mark will settle. And some just don't want to do business until they can be sure. . . . A senior partner of the big Hamburg export firm . . . tells . . . how negotiators were in the final stages of concluding a \$4.4 million agreement involving a glass-making factory for Zambia. 'The fountain pens were already drawn'. . . when Zambia's finance minister stepped in and declared that his country couldn't commit itself to any contract in marks. No other parties to the deal wanted to assume the currency risk, so it fell through. And an export manager at Volkswagen in Wolfsburg laments that 'the uncertainty is making business very difficult and in some cases nearly impossible'.[18]

After a five-day panicky closure of the exchanges, calm prevailed when the markets reopened. Speculators who had sold borrowed dollars to buy European currencies which they did not intend to use, were in the market to buy dollars to settle their accounts. The banking community was impatient to benefit from the floating through increased transaction charges and hedging.

> British companies with large overseas operations see the float as no more than a temporary aberration. . . . Yet foreign-exchange dealers in London have reacted well indeed to the new challenge. Why then are the custodians of the old system – the world's treasurers, central bankers, international civil servants of the International Monetary Fund – so dead set against floating? . . . Some finance ministers also have a horror that they will give up some political power if they allow the market, rather than themselves, to decide exchange rates. This is silly.[19]

The Economist was disappointed by the fact that British company treasurers, finance directors and accountants did not rush for cover to their bankers:

> most British companies . . . are abysmally ignorant about foreign exchange – and apparently intend to remain so. Such ignorance will be costly. Floating exchange rates mean uncertainty of the sterling profit on a transaction. Companies need certainty, and they can get it by obtaining their currency in advance in the forward market. . . . Foreign exchange departments of the clearing banks and merchant banks will obviously have to go out and teach their clients what it is.[20]

With the exception of the American and British press and banking community, everybody was perplexed and concerned. Even the Church lamented. *The Wall Street Journal* reported from the Vatican City:

> The Vatican weekly *Osservatore della Domenica*, in a rare comment on financial affairs, castigated 'parasitic' currency speculators for contributing to the present monetary crisis. 'The race to profits and get-rich-quick schemes have always existed, but as sick disorders in a substantially healthy body. Now they seem to have become an organic disease', said the commentary. 'It is, to be sure, a foolishly tragic illusion which brings to mind Midas. This accumulation of "wealth" is in the final analysis an impoverishment.'

While international trade was struggling with the problems of floating, Connally continued to harass the Europeans with new demands. On 15 September, at a Group of Ten meeting, he told the United States' trading partners that they must help produce a $13 billion improvement in the American balance of payments by revaluing their currencies against the dollar and by taking a larger share in defence commitments. American insistence on 'burden sharing' was to a large extent rhetoric. 'We had a problem and we're sharing it with the world, just like we shared our prosperity,' Connally said on television: 'That's what friends are for.'

American bankers and businessmen added their weight to press home the advantages gained by their government. At a meeting of the chief executives of 110 of the largest American and European corporations, in Versailles, the chairman of the First National Bank of Chicago warned the Europeans that the United States would take whatever action was necessary if the Common Market did not terminate and wind down its proliferation of preferential trade agreements with non-EEC countries and if it did not give more significant relief for United States agricultural products. Europe should also increase its share in the defence of the free world. 'We have a great deal of clout – that I hope we don't have to exercise,' he added.[21]

The Europeans felt unjustifiably injured by Nixon's protectionist measures, but equally helpless and reduced to venting their irritation. Pompidou accused Nixon of brandishing a big stick while possibly preparing some 'carrot' by promising to withdraw the 10 per cent surcharge on imports. 'France', he said, was not ready to 'play the role of the donkey'.[22]

Whenever United States politicians started talking tough, putting the Europeans on the defensive, they were rewarded with dissenting indecision.

Connally made an attempt to divide the Europeans by announcing that he was ready for a selective lifting of the import surcharge because Germany had permitted the mark to float upward. The French reacted by stating that this would probably wreck the Common Market. The Bonn government denied the existence of any agreement and indicated that it would seek a clarification of Connally's remarks.[23] 'I had a choice between being considered mysterious and being considered overbearing and demanding. I chose to be mysterious,' said Connally, in a facetious comment on the incident.[24]

Subjected to Connally's cavalier manners, the European finance ministers became used to being pushed around; they were relieved and even delighted every time Washington made a 'friendly' gesture.

Under-secretary of the Treasury, Paul Volcker, described the Group of Ten meeting chaired by Connally at the Palazzo Corsini in Rome on 1 December 1971 as 'the most interesting international meeting of my career'.[25]

The European finance ministers had opened the meeting by stating that there was nothing to discuss unless the United States devalued the dollar in terms of gold. 'All right, the issue has been raised,' said Connally. 'Let's assume ten percent. What will you people do?'

There was no answer, no discussion, no attempt to change the subject, no call for recess; for almost an hour, there was just silence. Some smoked, some whispered a little to their colleagues, some just fidgeted, but no one wanted to take the lead in addressing the meeting. Finally, it was Karl Schiller who spoke. Germany, given its concern about inflation and the strength of its external position, had long been the most flexible of our trading partners on exchange rate policy. . . . Germany would accept a realignment of twelve percent. . . . The Germans put their European partners on the spot. The British and the Italians protested their inability to participate in any significant realignment. The French remained quiet.[26]

Nixon chose to negotiate with the French, a nation of gold bugs. The French wanted to eliminate the dollar-based system and replace it with one based on gold.

In mid-December 1971 President Pompidou and his Finance Minister Giscard d'Estaing took a Concorde flight to the Azores to meet with President Nixon. France declared itself satisfied with an 8.6 per cent revaluation of the franc against the dollar and the United States agreed to raise the dollar-gold price from $35 to $38 an ounce.

The meeting in the Azores opened the way for the Smithsonian Agreement a few days later, where a general realignment took place and the United States achieved an average depreciation of about 8 per cent against all OECD (Organization for Economic Cooperation and Development) currencies. The dollar, however, remained inconvertible at the new price of $38 an ounce; the French seemed to be satisfied with this new price at which the United States would not sell its gold. The yen was revalued by nearly 17 per cent. Currencies would be allowed to fluctuate around wider bands of 2.25 per cent as opposed to the 1 per cent under the Bretton Woods Agreement. By widening the margins around the official rates, the distinction between fixed and floating rates tended to dissolve. Greeted hyperbolically as the greatest event in memory of monetary history, the Smithsonian Agreement would soon collapse under renewed attacks by currency speculators. The British float in June 1972 was the first formal break in the Smithsonian central rates. The Bank of England had spent roughly £1 billion to defend its currency and finally let the pound float.

Speculators were now on their way to victory. Ever increasing amounts of Eurodollars mounted an attack against the bastion of solidity, the Swiss franc. The Swiss national bank had been intervening to support the dollar, but finally decided to stop throwing good money after bad and let its franc float. By now the speculators had learned all the tricks of the game; the central banks had not. Smelling blood, currency dealers started another wave on 1 March 1973. Again the Bundesbank and other central banks spent almost $4 billion to defend the dollar and on 2 March the markets were closed once more for two weeks. When they reopened, all the currencies of the Western world were allowed to float.

The resort to floating in early 1973 was not taken out of any general conviction that it was a better system; it was simply a last resort when European countries realized they were unable to defend their currencies against speculation. In the terminology of the time, speculation was directed against the dollar, whereas in fact it was directed against the Bretton Woods system of fixed currencies.

Connally had become the symbol of the new American impatience with the rest of the world; his showdown tactics and style were widely applauded by the American press, but some people in the Administration thought he had gone too far and pushed too hard. The *New York Times* said:

The Treasury Secretary has opened an angry confrontation with the nation's allies – and so far, has avoided negotiation. . . . These unjustifiable demands and the effort to bludgeon the allies into surrender with an import surcharge that virtually doubles the American tariff, has led Connally into highly misleading attempts at justifying his tactics to the Congress and to American opinion as well as to the allies.[27]

Testifying before Congress, after being told that he had become a 'focal point of irritation', he answered amid laughter that disagreement with the allies could be met 'with good grace, reason and logic', and that 'a pearl starts as an irritation in an oyster'.[28]

Connally resigned in May 1972. He had emerged as the major figure in American politics. As for his European 'friends', he had promised to 'shake their heads together', and had observed: 'they're big boys now'. Much of the American press admired his 'extraordinary political intelligence and a conviction that the national interest – or at least the free enterprise system – begins with the interest of the nation's wealthy'.[29]

His successor, George P. Shultz, will be an unusual Secretary of the Treasury in that he is an academic economist rather than a banker and a man of wealth. In the past, the suggestion of an economist in that job has usually evoked great anxiety among bankers, who suspect that he would attempt to manage them rather than to represent them.[30]

Thus years of monetary turmoil came to an end; they had revolutionized world finance. A German banker observed that 'the European central banks, on close examination, are not much more than regional offices of the Federal Reserve, but without voting rights'.[31]

The submission to the dollar was virtually complete, unquestioned, undebated in any of the parliamentary assemblies where lesser but more obvious derogations of sovereignty would have met with howls of protest.

9 The Eurodollar

It's our currency but it's your problem.
John Connally

According to the usual definition a Eurodollar is a deposit denominated in United States dollars at any bank located outside of the United States, including a foreign branch of a United States bank.

The President of the Federal Reserve Bank of Boston formulated the American position as follows:

> Eurodollars are not dollars but *claims* on dollars which are created without the slightest evaporation from the pool of cash available to banks in the United States.
>
> Just as Eurodollars are not dollars, they also are not *money*, for money must serve as a means of payment as well as a store of wealth.[1]

Paul Einzig, expert and prolific writer on the subject, disagreed:

> The truth is that Euro-dollars are in no way different from ordinary dollars. They must be dollars held on deposit in the United States, with a bank resident in the United States. . . . This means that when an American bank borrows Euro-dollars in London, all that happens is that it increases its own deposits at the expense of some other American bank. . . . The total of American deposits held by the American banking system as a whole remains unaffected.[2]

Obviously, a definition of the Eurodollar has not yet become an integral part of the corpus of monetary theory. If it is private international money as the Americans claim, no legal framework exists to which one can refer to establish its properties. Obviously also, a definition is more than a subtle exercise in semantics.

Through what alchemy or what magic did some dollars deposited with a bank outside the United States cease to be dollars and cease to be *money*, to become *claims* on dollars? The question today is academic. Whatever definition and corollary theory one may decide upon, it would be devoid of feedback effects: the Eurodollar is here to stay, if not for ever, at least for some indefinite time to come.

This does not completely exclude that one day a financial cataclysm may spring a chain reaction that would shake the foundations of the banking system upon which the Eurodollar rests, and force the governments of the major trading nations to turn back the clock and bring the international monetary system back under their control. When, in a highly controversial domain, the most authoritative experts differ radically and dogmatically and build theories on self-interest or all-embracing faith, when innumerable publications on the subject are nothing more than mercenary literature, elementary prudence counsels looking elsewhere for enlightenment. The observation that in monetary affairs more can be learned from history than any other way applies also to the Eurodollar.

The Eurodollar revolution, the most significant monetary creation since the appearance of banknotes during the seventeenth century, unfolded subterraneanly. Its origin has been referred to by many writers, but was always glossed over, as if the obscure inception of this offshore and offshoot dollar was better left unmentioned and forgotten.

CONTRABAND DOLLARS IN PARIS

To find out how and where the Eurodollar came to life, we must go to Paris. In 1921 a few Russian exiles bought a small bank to serve their countrymen in France. They renamed it 'Banque Commerciale pour l'Europe du Nord' (BCEN). The venture failed and in 1925 the Russian state-owned Gosbank took it over, keeping most of the personnel.

After World War II the bank resumed its activities, operating like any other bank in the capitalist world. The cable address was 'EUROBANK'.

The BCEN soon became the largest foreign bank in France. It handled the international financial transactions of the Communist countries, from China to Poland, from Cuba to Rumania: commercial operations by the import–export organizations, airlines, embassies, press agencies and so on. It also handled the sale of Russian gold.

In addition, thousands of French clients used the services of the bank: everything connected with the French Communist party, then very powerful, dealt with the BCEN. Communist ministers, senators and deputies were paid directly by the French government through their accounts with the bank. Numerous private citizens, including much of the intelligentsia, had numbered accounts. It was an active and very prosperous bank.[3]

Shortly after the outbreak of the Korean war in June 1950, the Chinese government, fearing confiscation of its dollar assets, made a deposit of $5 million in a special account with the BCEN in the name of the Hungarian National Bank. The BCEN immediately decided to get rid of these dollars by relending them, thus ensuring a more secure protection. In order to establish contact, it lent them at slightly below-market rates to several French banks and to the Paris branch of the Bank of America.

Soon additional sums were deposited; the amounts increased to become a highly confidential but fast-growing parallel money market. Disguised as holdings of Paris-based banks, these dollars, in the hands of the Crédit Lyonnais, the Société Générale and the Bank of America, were lent out at rates slightly lower than current dollar rates. The first major borrowers were the dollar-hungry governments of Italy, Belgium, Holland and Britain. The French government used the funds to adjust its accounts with the European Payments Union (EPU). Thus Chinese-owned dollars were used for the reconstruction of Europe.

The cable address of the BCEN being 'EUROBANK', in the jargon of the banks using these dollars, they soon came to be called 'Eurodollars'. For the first time important transactions in dollars took place outside the United States without being subjected to American banking regulations or American interest rates. Moreover, as in any other banking system, additional Eurodollars could be created. The Chinese still owned them but the borrowers could use them. And the beauty of the whole operation was that no bureaucrat had put his nose into it and that no minimum reserve was required.[4]

The Banque de France must have known about it since the French government borrowed these dollars, and must have guessed that something unusual was going on, but apparently closed its eyes and ears preferring not to know.

In 1953, when the Korean war came to an end, the central banks of the communist world continued to channel their dollars through this new market, which had in the meantime, equally secretly, expanded to the London-based Moscow Narodny Bank. The legendary expertise of the City was now available for further expansion. The Eurodollar had the same value as the United States dollar. It was the medium of a new and separate, but somewhat illegitimate market where capitalist and communist banks could traffic in dollars without interference by any government. No one had planned it, no one authorized it and, except the banks involved in its operations, nobody cared to know about it.

For a decade this highly secretive and strange new money market continued to grow without attracting attention. There is a time lag between the inception of innovative banking practices and the perception of their impact on the economy. The origin of the Eurodollars was concealed by the fact that the bankers explained their existence as stemming from the

United States payments deficit. In 1959 *The Economist* referred to it in a brief article.

Later that year, when Paul Einzig stumbled by sheer accident upon something which he considered a back-door market, he set out to inquire among the practitioners. He recounts:

> The Euro-dollar market was for years hidden from economists and other readers of the financial Press by a remarkable conspiracy of silence. Bankers deliberately avoided discussing it with financial editors, presumably for fear that publicity might attract additional rivals to the market, or that it might breed criticism in the Press and opposition in official quarters. . . . When I embarked upon an inquiry on it in London banking circles, several bankers emphatically asked me not to write about the new practice, except perhaps in articles in learned journals or in my books which, they assumed, were in any case too technical for the uninitiated.[5]

The Eurodollar had its limitations: as long as it stayed in the Eurodollar banking chain it could not be used to withdraw gold from the Federal Reserve nor to pay a debt in the United States. It could, of course, always be converted into United States dollars.

As in any national banking system the deposit stood to the credit of the original depositor. But there were now also new deposits from the proceeds of the loans. Both deposits could be used to make payments.

Eurodollars had thus been created and the banks involved in the market could perform indefinitely the miracle of the fishes and the loaves without interference from any authority. It must be observed here that the term 'deposit' covers different realities and is to a certain extent a misnomer.

OFFSHORE DOLLARS IN THE CITY

After ten years of hiding, the Eurodollar market had now come into the open and was acclaimed by the Americans as an additional manifestation of the power of the dollar and in British banking circles as an unexpected and almost miraculous instrument to be used for the revival of the City as a financial centre.

The Continental central banks and governments had taken advantage of its low rates but were uncurious and seemingly unaware of the implications of the monetary revolution that was taking place on their soil and under their noses. Eurodollars were increasingly exchanged against national currencies and American companies used them to buy European companies or to establish new factories on the Continent.

At first sight the prospect of accumulating large quantities of dollars did not seem unpleasant; but when the mass of dollars started exceeding by far the amount of liquidity needed to finance trade and industry, the problem came out into the open. While governments put straitjackets on their monetary policies in order to keep a grip on inflation, dollars poured in freely and were exchanged against their own currencies.

The nucleus of a private international money market outside any government control, subject only to the strict rules of the banking community, had been established. Once injected into the bloodstream of the European economy, the Eurodollar developed a cancerous growth.

THE INTEREST EQUALIZATION TAX

The United States' exports exceeded by far its imports, but for several years the balance of payments was in deficit, mainly because American business had been investing heavily in Europe. In several countries they were more or less welcome; France's de Gaulle witnessed with dismay the passing of vital segments of its economy into foreign ownership and denounced it as exploitative. But since the Americans had the dollars, factory owners sold out; municipalities wishing to attract new factories to provide employment for their local labour force, subsidized their establishment.

The battle cry of American industry was: 'go to Europe'. When one company in a given industry made the move, the competitors felt they had to follow lest they be left behind. The herd instinct turned the exercise into a stampede. This was the time when United States papers described the beauty of foreign investment, much more profitable than domestic. In learned books and in the press the balance of payments theory was adapted to the circumstances: whatever its balance of payments, a creditor nation was a nation that invested abroad. The Webster sanctioned the new theory: in its 1965 edition it defined a creditor nation as 'a nation whose investments exceed in value the investments made in it by foreign countries'. This conveniently revised theory was expounded by American economists and became a leitmotiv in the American press, which made it credible to the public.

This was also the time of 'benign neglect' advocated by several leading economists and for a while adopted by the government, until the protests raised by the Europeans determined President Kennedy to make a gesture that would appease them.

Ever since his election he had expressed serious concern about the dollar drain which threatened the nation's gold supply. The balance of payments became one of his most publicized problems. Breaking with a well-established Democrat tradition, he had appointed an eminent Republican banker, C. Douglas Dillon, as Secretary of the Treasury. Under Republican presidents it was a well-established custom for pub- lic- spirited bankers to accept gladly a sizeable cut in salary for the privi- lege of serving the country, before returning to the banking community. Democrat presidents had generally appointed public servants or party politicians.

Robert V. Roosa, also closely associated with Wall Street, became Under-secretary and Paul Volcker was there to help him. Volcker had been at the Treasury before becoming David Rockefeller's assistant at Chase Manhattan.

In mid-1963 Roosa came up with the idea that the dollar drain could be stopped by levying a tax on medium- and long-term lending to for- eign borrowers. In official United States terminology any branch or sub- sidiary of an American company outside the United States is 'foreign'.

Roosa assigned Volcker to the task of working out the details. Volcker prepared a proposal which was immediately adopted by the Administra- tion: it was the interest equalization tax applicable to all medium- and long-term lending to 'foreign' borrowers. No tax was ever acclaimed with more enthusiasm by the inner circle of the banking community. It was indeed one of the most sophisticated pieces of economic diplomacy ever to come out of the United States Treasury.

Volcker called it an ingenious mimic. 'This provided an interesting les- son to me about government. It seemed an imaginative and intellectually attractive idea to simulate the market system without really using it.'[6]

The stated purpose of the tax was to limit the outflow of dollars, a seemingly-friendly move towards Europe. It had indeed become urgent to make a generous and altruistic gesture that would alleviate European anxieties.

The hidden purpose, which was not recognized nor understood by the Europeans, was the massive transfer of dollar lending in New York to Eurodollar lending in London, under the benevolent patronage of the Bank of England, outside the reach of any government supervision. Because of the fantastic potential it opened for American business abroad, it was welcomed with excitement – but, for obvious reasons, with muted trepidation by the American banking community:

Roosa said that a New York banker told him at the time that
'we'll make a fortune on this. We'll do all our dealings in dollars in
Europe.'[7]

When the tax was announced in the press it provoked a storm of protests
among the American business community in Europe. Volcker toured the
capitals on the Continent to explain the hidden facet: the tax only
applied to the head offices and not to the foreign branches. Things
calmed down immediately.

Roosa soon left the Treasury to make some money at a New York
investment bank. Volcker returned to Chase Manhattan as vice-president in charge of 'forward planning'.

The magic of national paper money which the goldsmith-bankers
discovered three hundred years ago was now made to work in the international money market, with an independent interest-rate structure, outside of national cartels and outside the control of any government or
central bank. Something entirely new, an institutional revolution.

The Interest Equalization Tax spawned the most massive banking
expansion in history, effectively transferring the global operational centre of the American banking system from the United States to London.
What they could not do at home they could do better in the City. Moreover, every reputable American bank was welcomed to set up a branch
without any capital, borrow in the interbank market and lend to its customers in Europe or anywhere else outside Britain.

In 1955 there were six American banks in London, carrying on modest
and routine activities. In 1970 they were 34. A London-based American
banker attributed the new prosperity of the City to 'good luck mixed with
good management'.

The greatest element of luck has been the institution of a series of measures by the US Government which has driven off-shore most dollar-
borrowing by foreigners, and most dollar-borrowing by US companies for use abroad. The City has been the principal beneficiary of the
business driven out of Wall Street. . . . Regulation Q, Interest Equali-
sation Tax, Department of Commerce Off-shore Direct Investment
Regulations and the Federal Reserve Voluntary Lending Limitations
are such important props to the London banking scene, they must certainly be acknowledged by anybody taking a view of the City. . . . The
Bank of England must take a large share of credit for this happy state
of affairs, but both the Labour and Conservative Governments have
given their central bankers solid support. The absence of local capital
requirements is certainly one of the attractive local features. Generous

and flexible tax treatment of foreign banks and bankers is another pleasant part of the City. . . . Regulation is minimal. This is not the result of inattention because the Old Lady knows as much and probably more than anyone about the Euromarket. It is a deliberate policy to let market forces control the market.[8]

Once again, things were not what they seemed. Europe, in search of its identity, its leadership diffuse and dispersed, where finance ministers are politicians but not financiers, with a starry-eyed Commission, unaware of the conundrums of international finance but convinced that the world will adjust to its elaborate plans, is no match for a dynastic Anglo-Saxon politico-financial establishment. These people understand money, they possess the technical knowledge and they stick together. They make mistakes, but they have for years helped their clients acquire astronomical quantities of goods and services, paying for them by papering the world with dollars. The grim faces of finance ministers and central bankers after each monetary crisis, or an occasional gnashing of teeth have no effect on the course of events. For better or for worse, by 1970, two decades after its inception, the Eurodollar market had established itself as the most highly efficient money market in the world, free from government intervention, offering breadth, convenience, low cost of doing business and interest rates set to suit the lender and the borrower; where credits could be raised and renewed quickly and with great ease, at favourable rates outside the national interest-rate cartels. Backed by a powerful economy and by the international primacy of the dollar, the bulk of the market remained concentrated in a dozen American banks in London, plus a few British banks.

It was estimated that Eurodollar positions amounted to $11.5 billion in 1965. Between 1969 and 1970 the size of the market jumped from $44 billion to $57 billion. By June 1972 it was at $82 billion. Occasionally the European countries tried to dampen the dollar flow, but without success. In the late 1960s the Group of Ten dreamed up a scheme involving the creation of IMF-sponsored Special Drawing Rights (SDRs) in the hope that the United States would play by the 'rules of the game' and use its SDRs to redeem unwanted dollars in the hands of other central banks.

As Otmar Emminger, deputy governor of the Bundesbank remarked, it was uncomfortable to be 'in bed with an elephant', but there was not much to be done about it. Not bound by the rules of play, the Americans became masters of the game, considering it a sacred right to do as they pleased. The Eurodollar introduced an entirely new element and dimension into the international financial structure with far-reaching implications.

The Eurodollar market thus became an important link and supplement to national markets, with a major difference: whereas most countries, particularly Germany, restricted the issue of their own money to the needs of the economy, Eurodollars were massively exchanged for national currencies, forced upon the central banks and added to the local money supply, undercutting anti-inflationary policies. The end-users must indeed exchange their Eurodollars for a local currency if they want to acquire goods or services.

The Bank of England was well aware of this: until the end of 1969 it was practically impossible for a British firm to obtain a licence to borrow Eurodollars. Harold Wilson, facing an election and saddled with a considerable balance of payments deficit, decided that an inflow of dollars – even stateless Eurodollars – would improve the image of his government.

SIR SIEGMUND G. WARBURG: INVENTOR OF THE EUROBOND

While nobody ever claimed paternity of the Eurodollar, because of its bastard and very dubious origin, Siegmund Warburg was the proud inventor of the Eurobond. He had closed his bank in Hamburg in 1933, when Hitler came to power, and had established a new bank in London. He had been active in the Eurodollar market and in 1962 he observed, like everyone else, that long-term borrowing in New York had become difficult and expensive. A lot of money was circulating in the rapidly growing Eurodollar system, separately from the dollar deposits. No law prohibited the issue of securities denominated in Eurodollars although it had not been done. The climate seemed favourable. The new Secretary of the Treasury, Douglas Dillon, had repeatedly recommended that American companies established in Europe borrow in the Eurodollar market.

During a visit to Washington, Warburg was told by friends at the World Bank that the market had grown to about $3 billion. This money, he thought, could be used for long-term lending. He learned that an Italian company, Finsider, a subsidiary of the state-owned IRI, was considering a very substantial investment, but had no capital available. He sent an associate to Rome to offer a loan, but Istituto per la Ricostruzione Industriale (IRI) refused: Finsider had financial problems and would not be able to guarantee repayment. 'Never mind,' said Warburg: 'we will lend the money to another IRI subsidiary, for instance the very profitable Autostrade; and since the Italian government guarantees the loan, there is no problem.'

He decided to issue the bonds in Luxembourg where the duties were almost nil. The contract signed in The Hague on 1 July 1963, made up according to English law, covering a $15 million loan, stipulated that the bonds would be issued by a Luxembourg bank to finance the investments in lire of an Italian company; the real borrower was not mentioned in the contract. Warburg's commission amounted to 3.5 per cent.

The issue created an enormous surprise and the response was very unfavourable. Then a miracle happened: on 18 July 1963 the Kennedy Administration announced the Interest Equalization Tax, which made borrowing in New York practically impossible. The financial centre for dollar borrowing moved from New York to London.

In the history of banking, every age has produced a few minds permeated with the quintessence of the art: precursors, trailblazers, harbingers of the possible and the probable, accelerators of the evolutionary process. Siegmund Warburg had such a mind.

He then undertook a tour of the European central banks.

In London, Bonn, Rome, Paris, he tells every central bank governor: 'it is not because New York is closed that we are going to let the international capital market die. Companies must be able to borrow without your having to create money. The dollars will come out anyway . . . instead of preventing the outflow of dollars from the United States the tax is going to increase it. The best for you is to permit the issue of long-term dollar loans.'[9]

It was not easy; some of the central bankers did not like these stateless dollars. He finally convinced everyone, warning that if the market did not develop, the financing of the American multinationals would dry up. He wrote down in his notebook: 'sometimes obstacles constitute a challenge to find new ways'. After a difficult start and considerable speculative losses by the initial investors, the Eurobond market was to become the most important long-term loan market. Warburg had argued it into existence.

Euromarket credits are based primarily on the reputation and the confidence enjoyed by the borrower, while classical loans require the borrower to convince the bank of his creditworthiness by submitting his balance, proving his need for capital, giving detailed information on the project to be financed and, frequently, providing collateral.

The Eurocurrency market has no authority to watch over its excesses and no lender of last resort. No single country is responsible for its soundness. In a national money market the central bank tries to control growth and stands ready to prevent a sudden contraction of credit. Ultimately, the stability of the market depends on the judgment, prudence and self-discipline of those who participate in it. It has weathered many crises and has survived.

The Eurodollar crushed Bretton Woods and 'suspended' the European Monetary System. These victories deliver day after day enormous dividends in transaction and hedging charges, creaming off the profits of industry. They have made advance planning considerably more difficult. Since August 1993 all European currencies are floating. The market operators are satisfied: they have absolute control over currency parities.

Logically, the world's largest debtor nation could not forever remain the home of the world's largest banks. In terms of capitalization, the most important financial institutions today are Japanese. Tokyo, despite its relative underdevelopment and the secrecy clouding its banking system, is becoming one of the epicentres of the world's money market. The dealers closest to the heaviest currency flows and to market volatility are no more in London or in Wall Street but in Asia. Could it be that a financial earthquake shaking Japan would send shock waves around the world, with unforeseeable consequences?

In December 1994 Japanese central banker Yasushi Mieno publicly stated that Japan's whole financial system had been 'in mortal danger' because two small banks failed and had to be bailed out by public funds from the Finance Ministry and the Tokyo city government.[10]

Two months later disaster struck Barings, the oldest merchant bank of the City. Steeped in tradition and regarded as a paradigm of prudence and conservatism, it suddenly collapsed. Reckless speculation in the highly profitable but risky derivatives market by the senior trader of its Singapore office wiped out in a few days the assets accumulated by generations of successful banking. An independent merchant bank, Barings blew up nothing much except itself. If a very large deposit-taking institution went bankrupt under similar circumstances, causing a chain reaction of insolvencies, the world financial markets could be subjected to systemic strains and disruptions of a much more serious nature.

10 Europe Unite

More than anywhere else the trauma of two world wars and of the Great Depression had produced in Europe a profound desire for a world where nationalism would recede and be replaced by international economic and political cooperation.

In the late 1940s some 200 bilateral trade agreements had been signed between the European governments. Each of them specified the quantities of goods that could be exchanged between two trading partners. All governments used exchange controls and import restrictions to balance their accounts with every other country, because any deficit had to be paid in gold or dollars.

Britain intended to maintain its traditional role as a major financial world power and to re-establish the role of sterling as a reserve and trading currency. The first requirement would be to make the pound convertible into gold. Bretton Woods had put the dollar at the centre of a new monetary system. When, in 1947, Britain implemented its intention, the European central banks rushed in to acquire sterling balances and convert them into dollars. The experiment lasted six weeks.[1]

Early in June 1947, Secretary of State General Marshall, returning from Moscow, had become convinced that Stalin would not relinquish his control of Eastern Europe, but that he was intent on westward expansion with the help of the Communist parties of France and Italy. In his famous Harvard address, Marshall stated the unpleasant but obvious fact that Europe needed goods from America and was unable to pay. Unless the United States provided help over a period of four years, after which Europe would have to become self-sufficient, substantial political, economic and social dislocations were to be expected. The Marshall Plan was led by Paul Hoffman, president of the Studebaker Corporation.

In April 1948, in response to the self-help commitment Marshall had suggested, the Organisation for European Economic Cooperation (OEEC) was established. Member countries agreed to 'achieve as soon as possible a multilateral system of payments among themselves and . . . [to] cooperate in relaxing restrictions on trade and payments between one another'. American aid was planned to decline gradually; each time the beneficiaries were presented with the reduced allocations, they denounced as unfair the restrictions imposed upon them. The negotiations about Marshall Aid produced 'more argument than agreement' and the OEEC efforts 'more machinery than results'.[2]

Fortunately, a few statesmen such as Schuman, de Gasperi and Adenauer nurtured the dream of unifying Europe through a voluntary merger of sovereignty of the various nation states. Jean Monnet gave the idea its economic dimension. The industrial performance and the living standards of the United States came to be attributed to the size of its market and the free flow of goods and money between its vast borders. If similar conditions could be established in Europe, a better division of labour and a more efficient use of the human and material resources would greatly improve the well-being of its population.

These concepts were rejected by the British authorities. They had successfully opposed French efforts to give the OEEC considerable power and prerogatives: the organization should not make policy decisions but should remain under the control of the various governments. 'We should not embark on a policy of cooperation on the assumption we were ready to extricate the other countries from their difficulties at the cost of sacrificing ourselves. But we should be prepared to initiate a policy of multilateralism and take some risks.' A memo issued by the Foreign Office and the Treasury in October 1949 defined British policy as 'one under which His Majesty's Government were not to involve themselves in the economic affairs of Europe beyond the point from which they could, if they wished, withdraw'.[3]

Intra-European trade expanded gradually, largely as a result of rising production levels, mainly in Germany. Paul Hoffman was persuaded that Europe would not be viable by the end of the four-year Marshall Plan unless steps were taken toward economic integration, which he saw as a prelude to political integration. He lectured the European governments, asking them to work out concrete plans to make Europe a single market as soon as possible. British officials kept insisting on including Europe in the sterling area by using the pound when offsetting their mutual balances.

It was an American, Richard M. Bissell, assistant administrator of the Marshall Plan, who took the initiative in December 1949 to submit a proposal for an Intra-European Clearing Union: based on Keynes' ideas, the Union would establish transferability between all Western European countries. After prolonged and often heated debate between the Europeans themselves, the American proposals were incorporated into the European Payments Union agreement.

Camille Gutt, Managing Director of the International Monetary Fund, expressed grave concern, considering that the EPU would challenge his responsibilities and authority. Chancellor Cripps objected because the European clearing system was irreconcilable with the sterling area. The 'prestige of sterling' was a leitmotiv in the London memoranda. Britain, wed to the Commonwealth, the sterling area and a 'special relationship' with the United States, considered the Continent as more a liability than a contributor. As usual, perceptions of national interest, whether founded or misguided, real or imaginary, dominated the negotiations.

Six countries soon began negotiating the Coal and Steel Community that would later become the Common Market. Germany's role was restrained; its representatives tried to gain acceptance and avoided any controversy with France, still apprehensive of admitting Germany to full status in a European organization.

After long and heated debate and a number of prolonged impasses and hurdles, Britain always insisting on a special status for sterling, to the extent that on a number of occasions its participation seemed doubtful, finally on 7 July 1950 the OEEC ministers decided to establish the EPU.

THE EUROPEAN PAYMENTS UNION

A radically new payments system was thus created between 17 European countries. Responsibility for the technical operations concerning debts and credits was delegated to the Bank for International Settlements. The concept of EPU was more or less a carbon copy of Bretton Woods.

Germany provoked the first crisis. At the outbreak of the Korean war, in June 1950, the fear of raw-material shortages pushed German industry to participate heavily in the international buying wave; Economics Minister Ludwig Erhard had made Germany the spearhead in the move to reduce restrictions in international trade and currency convertibility. Concerned that Germany was buying excessive amounts of raw materials, the American High Commissioner John J. McCloy threatened to reimpose trade controls. The Bundesbank decided to restrict bank credit by increasing its discount rate from 4 to 6 per cent. Chancellor Adenauer – who, incidentally, was John McCloy's brother-in-law – argued that this would undermine reconstruction; he put heavy pressure on the Bank to cancel the decision. The council members refused to listen. In the eyes of the German public the Bundesbank became the reliable guardian of the D-mark.[4]

Ever since the end of the war the Germans had kept a low profile. The EPU was the first organization to treat them as equals. At the end of the war it seemed for a while that Germany would require several decades to rebuild its economy. Once more hyperinflation had completed the destruction wrought by war. This was the time when 'in Germany we calculated that the average German would be able to buy a plate every five years, a pair of shoes every twelve years and a suit every fifty years'.[5]

Cigarettes and coffee were the most widely coveted means of payment in the black market. On Sunday, 20 June 1948, all notes and coins were declared worthless. The Germans stood in line to receive 40 new D-mark each; employers received 60 D-mark per employee. All money claims, all bank deposits and mortgage bonds were reduced to a tenth of their nominal value. The American occupation forces had established the Bank deutscher Länder headed by Wilhelm Vocke and other former Reichsbank officials. The new D-mark did not seem to have much of a future. Vocke recounts:

> In 1949 . . . I visited an important foreign central bank and one of the leading directors – a good friend of mine – told me between four eyes: 'The German mark is not a currency, it will not become a currency and cannot become a currency. It's not a currency, it's a bad joke.' These were hard words. At the end of the year Mr. Gutt, head of the International Monetary Fund, whom I knew well, invited me for the first time again to visit the United States. When I talked to him he said: 'Now, Mr Vocke, no gold, no currency reserves, I must tell you honestly, you haven't got a chance, the D-mark can never amount to anything.'[6]

Contrary to all expectations, within a few years, Erhard's policy supported by a national consensus to work harder for less money than anybody else, led the German economy to the 'miracle' and to the convertibility of the currency. Within two years Germany became the Union's largest creditor.

Throughout the decade of the 1950s Europe's productivity, consumption, investment and employment reached new heights year after year. Though reluctant to join the system, the United Kingdom was a major early beneficiary of the EPU arrangements. France, involved in a war in Indo-China and subject to political instability and social strife, accumulated deficits and, in February 1952, completely suspended trade liberalization while severely tightening foreign exchange controls.

In the United States, despite the fact that American officials had taken the initiative of proposing the EPU, powerful groups in the Treasury and the State Department were against it. 'The US should oppose any action by the Union favoring measures to impose discriminatory restrictions on transactions with the dollar area.'[7]

As Europe recovered and became prosperous, one currency after the other became convertible, though not without recurrent crises, admirably described in the book on which this chapter is based. Conceived at the end of 1949, the EPU was liquidated at the end of 1958, having accomplished its purpose. During its ten-year existence it freed European trade and payments from the bilateralist straitjacket and the import restrictions. It was the most effective and successful international organization created after the war, a mechanism that worked. It had demonstrated the benefits of economic integration to the peoples and the governments of Western Europe.

The mistakes of Versailles and its sequels had been avoided. The Morgenthau plan, presented by Harry White to General Eisenhower in August 1944, designed to reduce Germany for decades to a powerless agrarian state by flooding all its mines and destroying whatever was left of its industry, was only considered briefly by the American Administration. 'If I had my way, I would keep Germany on a breadline for the next twenty-five years,' Roosevelt reportedly told Morgenthau. Once the fight for survival was over, however, the plan died of neglect:

And while Morgenthau, back in Washington, remained convinced that a severe policy should be pursued in every phase of life in Germany, the occupation troops couldn't be interested in anything except getting along as comfortably as they could with the people they now had to live with . . . and found it quite possible to intensely dislike the German people, without at all disliking any particular German individual.[8]

Having escaped the fate programmed by the United States Treasury, Europe developed into a prosperous continent, with the help of the Marshall Plan. European governments were learning to live and work together, solving problems, resolving disagreements, compromising by reluctantly making concessions whenever necessary. The concepts of 'convergence' and 'coordination' were not yet part of the vocabulary, but national policies were increasingly adjusted with consideration for their effect on the trading partners. The fundamental idea of European integration, the primary instrument for accelerating Europe's economic recovery, was making progress. The major problems resolved by the EPU no longer existed, and their solution had strengthened the common bonds.

Interdependence and the awareness of its importance had grown considerably over the past decade. It became possible now to go a step further. The long period of currency stability under the Bretton Woods system had nourished the illusion that some sort of monetary union already existed. Several years of monetary turbulence in the 1960s and early 1970s had shaken the belief, but it seemed that a well-conceived plan would restore stability.

THE WERNER PLAN

Making Western European currencies freely convertible into United States dollars was one of the purposes and one of the achievements of the European Payments Union. The transitional period provided for in article XIV of the Bretton Woods Agreement had come to an end. The European countries were now able to trade under the rules and regulations of the International Monetary Fund: fixed exchange rates, stable without rigidity and flexible without looseness were the foundation of the system. The 'golden sixties' will be remembered as the most remarkable decade of sustained economic growth in history.

When Bretton Woods broke down in the early 1970s, after three years of currency speculation fuelled by the Eurodollar, the European governments started looking for a new monetary system of fixed exchange rates that would allow them to trade among themselves without the inconveniences resulting from unpredictable currency fluctuations. Floating exchanges have practically no impact on the vast and self-sufficient American economy. They posed grave problems to the European economy and constituted a major obstacle to further European integration. A common market is incompatible with volatile and unpredictable exchange rates. When the system of fixed but adjustable rates collapsed, the European governments immediately set out to create a regional zone of monetary stability. The prime minister of Luxembourg, Pierre Werner, was charged with the study of a plan that would promote European monetary union.

From the beginning there were two schools of thought: those who believed that a monetary union could only be the crowning achievement of political union, and the other school, which said that monetary policy could be used as a tool for accelerating the coordination of economic policy.

Werner thought that coordination in economic matters was a day-to-day business that would take time, whereas a monetary approach would be very precise and produce definite results within a short period of time. Monetary union would promote political union. The national economies, fiscal policy, credit supply, bank liquidity, interest rate structures, and so on, would have to be brought in line by mutual agreement. The first three-year stage had to be pragmatic and experimental.

In October 1970 the Werner Committee presented a plan for a monetary union to be accomplished by 1980: the Community currencies would be irreversibly linked and made convertible with immutable parity rates or, preferably, be replaced by one Community currency: monetary and credit policies were to be centralized; the Community would have jurisdiction over policy relations with the outside world; essential features of national budgets would be decided at Community level. The creation of two institutions would be necessary: one for the decisions on a common economic policy, and a Community central bank along the lines of the Federal Reserve System.

There was general agreement about the objectives, but sharp disagreements about the means and methods to be adopted. Germany wanted to start with coordinated consistent policy objectives. France insisted on narrower margins, the pooling of reserves, extended credit facilities and financial assistance. The French view prevailed. One of the weaknesses of the Werner Plan was that it took a Bretton-Woods-like system for granted, despite the fact that it had been completely shattered and proven very vulnerable.

The decision by the British government, on 23 June 1972, to allow sterling to float, after losing $2.5 billion in reserves in a six-day battle with currency speculators, was a heavy blow to the strategy of the Werner Plan even before it became operational.

On 26 June, after closing their exchange markets, the other EC countries decided to stick to existing agreements and to shelve for the time being the grandiose plans for a monetary union. The Anglo-Saxon banking community had won another battle rather easily. While the United States government simulated interest in international monetary reform by presenting a Volcker Plan to be discussed in the Committee of Twenty, the speculators kept up the pressure, repeatedly forcing the European central banks to close the markets, causing devaluations and revaluations, and in the process making huge and easy windfall profits.

THE SNAKE IN THE TUNNEL

On 7 March 1972, following the Smithsonian Agreement, which briefly restored a semblance of monetary stability by repegging currencies within 4.5 per cent, the countries belonging to the European Community signed the 'Snake' agreement.

Countries participating in the Snake had to keep their currencies within margins determined by a parity grid: each was assigned a bilateral central rate with every other currency and was allowed to fluctuate around this rate within a 2.25 per cent margin. If and when a pair of currencies reached these outer limits, the central banks in each country were required to intervene until the situation was corrected. The six Community members inaugurated the system in April 1972. They were soon joined by Britain, Ireland, Norway and Denmark. A wave of dollar-supported speculation forced Britain to leave the Snake within eight weeks of its adherence. Shortly afterwards the lira was forced to leave and the D-mark was revalued by 3 per cent. Later the guilder and the Norwegian krone were revalued and in January 1974 the French franc came under pressure and had to leave the system.

Despite these drawbacks, which prompted the governments to abandon the 1980 target for the European Monetary Union (EMU), efforts were repeatedly made to strengthen the Snake. In 1975 France linked the franc to the Snake again but was forced to opt out the following year. The causes of the failures and disappointments were several; many of the officials who devised the plan, and who had to implement it in the central banks, considered the timing premature. Some political leaders were unwilling to accept the political and institutional consequences of a union. There were also deep disagreements in the face of the global inflation coupled with recession. In Germany two hyperinflations had left deep scars and an independent Bundesbank was the guardian of the D-mark. In France and Italy monetary policy was determined by politicians and inflation had become a way of life.

Then there was the dollar problem: most European governments had meekly accepted United States financial domination; in fact submission was virtually complete. Britain, because of the profits this brought to the City, was all in favour. When de Gaulle protested against the confiscatory acquisition of French industry by American companies paying with paper dollars, when he repeatedly called gold back from Fort Knox, he became the *bête noire*, the *Gaullefinger*. He was universally condemned in the United States press for his irresponsible defiance and for forgetting that France had been saved from being defeated in two wars. Television showed a New York restaurateur emptying a bottle of expensive French wine into the gutter.

Germany, for understandable reasons, had made a virtue of necessity. The Bundesbank had opted for floating exchange rates as a lesser evil:

as long as the Bretton Woods Agreements were in operation, it had been forced to buy, against its will, billions of speculative Eurodollars. This had resulted in a much dreaded imported inflation, since the dollars were exchanged against D-marks and added to the money supply. The Americans said: 'We don't have inflation, so we cannot export it.' In Germany the subject was politically taboo though much criticized in the press. The Bundesbank had become the suffering but consenting *Prügelknabe* of the American bankers. In 1958 Karl Blessing had succeeded W. Vocke as president of the Bundesbank and had taken over a stable currency. But when speculative Eurodollars flooded the German market, the Bundesbank was forced to buy unlimited quantities until, repeatedly, it was able temporarily to stop speculation by revaluing or floating, leaving the speculators with substantial profits and the German economy with an oversupply of money.

Shortly before his death in 1971, Blessing, who had never openly accused the Americans, explained to *Der Spiegel* why things had gone so far. Because other European countries had chosen the path of inflation, which he did not want, he had been forced, under the pressure of speculators, to revalue the mark several times. 'We have in fact a dollar standard,' he said.

Spiegel: Yes, certainly, but aren't we considerably helping the Americans – including yourself when you were president of the Bundesbank – by holding American Treasury certificates, by accumulating their dollars and by not converting the dollars into gold?

Blessing: Yes, we did. I can tell you today that I feel guilty for this. I should have been much more rigorous with the Americans. We should simply have exchanged for gold all the dollars we accumulated.

Spiegel: And because of the inaction of the central banks the Americans have never been forced to solve their dollar problem.

Blessing: No, they have never been forced. They always promised us: 'next year things will change, and the year after next our budget and everything else will be in order. We are strong.' And as a trading nation they are. But they never succeeded; something always came in between. Then came the Vietnam war and President Johnson with his financial policy, with a 25-billion-dollar budget deficit in one year. All this caused inflation. I often told my American colleagues: 'it's always the same with you'. Then there was this business with the troops.

Spiegel: You mean the threat by the Americans: if you don't support the dollar this way, we will withdraw our troops from the Federal Republic?

Blessing: It was not a clearly stated menace, but the threat was always present in the background. The former high commissioner McCloy one day told the German government: 'Listen, we have a decision by the Senate and we are going to have a majority that wants to withdraw our boys. We have to do something. He then called me at home on a Sunday afternoon at half past three and said: 'I must fly back tonight, can we get together?' And I told him: 'My dear McCloy, your situation is clear, you have a payments problem, nothing else. You have seen that we are reasonable and that we don't convert our dollars into gold. I am even ready to confirm this in writing for a certain period of time.' Unfortunately, the letter I then wrote is still valid today.[9]

The former high commissioner McCloy was long-time chairman of the Chase bank. Blessing never mentioned the Eurodollar problem. Wilhelm Vocke thought his successor had judgment, experience and knowledge; but he was too good-hearted: 'He couldn't say no. His life also had its tragic side.'[10]

Conscious of the need for stable currencies within Europe, the Six embarked on a programme of economic and monetary union in the spring of 1971. The fate of the Snake was a clear indication of the disparity between European currencies. The Werner Plan had prematurely sought to impose a monetary union; as the Snake progressed, the need for economic policy coordination and for rapid progress in harmonizing the national rates of inflation became more and more evident. No plan, however ingeniously conceived, could bypass this basic rule. The rigid linking of currencies without very rapid progress in the harmonization of national inflation rates at a very low level was liable to be a source of monetary and economic strain.

MR SCHMIDT HAD A DREAM

The Treaty of Rome called for the creation of a European capital market by 1977 but did not specifically mention the objective of a monetary union. By 1970 the original goal of establishing a customs union and a common agricultural policy had been achieved. Europe had become commercially integrated, and needed a plan for monetary integration.

The Werner Plan had been torpedoed by a speculative assault even before it had become operational. After the Bretton Woods monetary system collapsed in the early 1970s, it had been replaced by the short-lived Smithsonian Agreement; Europe faced a very serious problem of monetary anarchy.

Americans enjoy the benefit of a massive, self-sufficient and integrated market stretching from the Atlantic to the Pacific. International trade is a minor part of their total economy. Europe was divided into many separate entities with floating currencies, a grave impediment to trade and advanced planning.

Under the Smithsonian Agreement the rates were allowed to fluctuate between margins of 2.25 per cent on either side of their parities against the dollar, so that the rate between any two could vary by $4\frac{1}{2}$ per cent from their cross-parity. This provided insufficient security for intra-European trade. In 1972 the six Common Market countries signed an agreement whereby they committed themselves to maintaining their currencies within 2.25 per cent from their cross-parities. It was called the 'Snake in the tunnel'. The Snake came immediately under attack from the speculators: Britain was not a member of the EEC at the time, but had joined the Snake very soon after its inception; a wave of currency speculation against the pound ended its brief membership. Denmark and Norway were also admitted.

In 1977 the European Community was drifting along, when Roy Jenkins became president of the Commission. Determined to revitalize the debate about economic and monetary integration, he engaged in a one-man crusade to persuade policy-makers that a common monetary policy was necessary to overcome the problems of growing unemployment, varying rates of inflation and economic divergence. The Snake would continue its existence but a closer relationship with non-Snake members had to be established.

In a speech to the European Parliament he declared that in a monetary union 'two of what are generally regarded as the more important functions of a modern government – control over the exchange rate and control over the money supply – would be exercised by a central Community institution instead of by governments'.[11]

He was convinced that a monetary union had to be a complete construction from the start: a half-way house would sooner or later collapse. The plan was faced with a serious obstacle: Community decision-making was neither national nor supranational, but rather, an ambiguous amalgam of both.

The reaction to the publication of Mr Jenkins' proposals was overwhelmingly negative. Within the Commission some were enthusiastic; others downright sceptical. Mr Ortoli, vice-president of the Commission and responsible for monetary policy, openly declared at a press conference that he considered Mr Jenkins' ideas 'politically absurd'. The German Finance Minister, Apel, ridiculed the proposal as nonsense. A British paper described the plan as 'at best a distant goal, at worst sheer folly'. Jenkins was, for better or for worse, a dreamer.

Mr Jenkins then decided to change his strategy and resort to high-level secret diplomacy. He knew that the French President, Giscard d'Estaing, was in favour of a zone of monetary stability and that Chancellor Schmidt shared the idea. In December 1977 the European Council noted with satisfaction the Commission's communication on European Monetary Union and requested a thorough study. Against overwhelmingly sceptical expert opinion, Chancellor Schmidt decided that a monetary union was essential for the future development of the Community. The odds were against Mr Jenkins' public statements and Mr Schmidt's secret dream: the Chancellor's contacts with his finance ministry and with the Bundesbank had convinced him that his initiative aroused considerable opposition and that he would consequently have to move forward without and against expert advice. During a meeting with the French President it was agreed that both would develop the idea at a European Council meeting in Copenhagen on 7 and 8 April 1978.

> The German chancellor, who was the last of the four major figures to speak . . . agreed with those who had preceded him. As far as he was concerned the most pressing problems lay elsewhere, in the shortcomings of the international monetary system and the inadequacies of the present American administration, which made these defects still worse. He recalled that when he and the French president had been finance ministers earlier in the 70s, they had already tried to devise defences against the immense increase in international liquidity and in particular against the threat presented by the Eurodollar market. If the situation had been bad then, it was catastrophic now and it had been made much more dangerous by the policies of the United States' administration. The Germans, he declared, could not go on buying dollars. When Mr Callaghan intervened to ask what alternative he saw to propping up the American currency, Mr Schmidt replied that it would simply have to be allowed to fall.[12]

Chancellor Schmidt's speech caused a surprise, since he had been an ardent defender of flexible rates at previous summit meetings, including the 1977 London summit. Germany had opted for floating exchanges as a lesser evil. The French President was even more emphatic: if the United Kingdom or any other country could not join the new system, Europe, which was at a crossroads, would split and France would rejoin the Snake.

It became evident that Mr Callaghan and Mr Andreotti were very worried. Chancellor Schmidt then revealed the most important features of the plan: the creation of a European Monetary Fund, the partial pooling of official reserves, the increased use of European Community currencies rather than dollars in intervention on the exchange markets and the creation of a European unit of account. President Giscard d'Estaing added that the proposal amounted to a 'new Bretton Woods for Europe'.

Most participants were reticent. Mr Callaghan expressed concern about the effect the plan might have on the dollar and on the position of the IMF. The plan was not directed against the dollar, said Mr Schmidt; but Mr Callaghan was not reassured and expressed annoyance at the way in which the plan had suddenly been sprung upon him.

When the plan was leaked to officials in the finance ministries and central banks, the reaction was mixed. To many experts it seemed that somebody was putting the cart before the horses. The Committee of Central Bank Governors was openly hostile: the plan was premature. The economic policies and priorities as well as the performances of the member states were too disparate. A coordinated monetary, fiscal and wage policy should come first; the plan did not foresee any institutional arrangements to guarantee such policy coordination. A new mechanism for linking the exchange rates required more effective measures to coordinate monetary and economic policies. A simple return of all Community countries to the Snake would be preferable.

For months the plan was discussed in numerous bilateral and multilateral expert committees, each separately and in secret, germinating divergent ideas with the result that differences of opinion ended up in disputes. Chancellor Schmidt became convinced that if the plan were left in the hands of central bank and finance ministry officials, it would be undermined and finally killed. It was necessary to entrust it to technically competent special advisers who had his confidence and who shared his views. The new Franco-German plan was to be revealed at a summit meeting in Bremen. The system would be new and different from the Snake.

In a remarkably open interview with *Business Week*, the Chancellor explained:

I'm not so much thinking in terms of enlarging the Snake, but of something which goes a little beyond the present Snake. I am thinking in terms of pooling some currency reserves. I'm thinking about a EUA that would also be the medium in which you settle accounts between the European Central Banks. I could imagine additional instruments of monetary assistance, of broadening the existing instruments and extrapolating them into the long range field. Of course there are . . . some risks. . . . It might mean for Germany . . . that we have to sacrifice some of our reserves. It might also mean that we have to expand our money supply somewhat more rapidly than we have done until now.[13]

The risks were evident: in the face of the enormous mass of speculative Eurodollars, any exchange-rate system requiring the systematic intervention of central banks to defend their currencies in order to maintain them within prescribed margins, has a built-in weakness that makes its survival unlikely. The determination to create something new could not conceal the important differences between German and French plans. The most controversial topic was the ECU. The French estimated that the ECU (an English acronym for the European Currency Union and also the name of an old French coin) would be at the centre of the Exchange Rate Mechanism, not just as numeraire but as the currency upon which the system would be based. The Germans doubted its technical feasibility. British representatives were definitely opposed but continued to participate in the discussions, although they were convinced their government would not join. The dollar had established London again at the centre of world finance and was providing fabulous profits to the City. Anything that might challenge the supremacy of the dollar had to be rejected. Anglo-Saxon common financial interests must prevail over European construction. Treasury forecasts of the probable consequences for the United Kingdom were apocalyptic, almost hysterical, predicting catastrophe if the government was deprived of its power freely to allow the pound to drift down should the need arise.[14]

Shortly after the conclusion of the Bremen Council meeting the British Prime Minister, Mr Callaghan, held a press conference. *The Times* reported:

There is considerable resentment at what is seen as the success of the German government in presenting its national interest as being a move for the greater good of Europe. . . . The fact that the whole thing is dealt with in just a few hundred words is generally felt to show the danger of allowing enthusiastic amateurs to dream up schemes of monetary reform.[15]

The Italians were not in the Snake and had not been involved in the negotiations; they resented their exclusion. Within the Italian administration many were hostile to any attempt to bring the lira back into a fixed exchange-rate system. The Dutch disapproved of the procedure, whatever the merit of the plan, and demanded to be consulted. The Belgians insisted that progress on essential issues was more important than the dispute about procedures, but expressed dislike about the way the whole affair had been handled.

The American administration had observed from a distance but with considerable interest the monetary negotiations in Europe. Some saw in it a sinister threat to American interests and supremacy: only the dollar should remain the pivot of the international monetary system. A United States Treasury spokesman expressed scepticism:

> Concerns about the possible effects of exchange-rate instability have spawned suggestions which focus on efforts to achieve greater stability through financial means, including exchange rate zones supported by massive official intervention, greatly expanded credit arrangements, foreign currency borrowing by the US and 'substitution' arrangements to stabilise official currency reserves. Such proposals treat the symptoms rather than the causes of present economic problems. Experience of the past decade has demonstrated repeatedly that exchange rate stability cannot be imposed on the system but must be the result of sound domestic policies.[16]

British aloofness was part of its imperial and commonwealth heritage. Having become again the world's financial centre, thanks to the Eurodollar, a European monetary union never seemed necessary nor desirable. Moreover, fixed exchange rates would enormously curtail the profits of the City. The traditional balance-of-power policy did not work any more and the feeling of a privileged relation with America – the source of the revival of the City – increased the feeling of insularity in all parties, reluctant to surrender part of national sovereignty. The Free Trade Association had been an attempt to enjoy the advantages of free trade without political commitments. With an economy in a state of stagnation, Britain had reluctantly requested entry into the EEC and, after much opposition from de Gaulle, been admitted.

During the meetings of the European Council at Bremen, on 6 and 7 July 1978, Schmidt and Giscard d'Estaing, two extremely self-conscious politicians, tried hard to obtain support for their proposals. Amidst protests by smaller countries that they had been excluded from the negotiations and did not understand the plan, the British Prime Minister continued to display strong reluctance about entering into such a commitment. After hours of coaxing and cajoling, the Council members were finally persuaded reluctantly to set aside their objections and to accept the Franco-German document as the basis for a detailed drafting by the Community experts, 'at the greatest possible speed'. Expert discussion should be finished by the end of October. The period of secret diplomacy had come to an end; the proposals were out in the open.

The plan was now put in the hands of three committees: the Monetary Committee, the Committee of Central Bank Governors and the Economic Policy Committee. The Bundesbank expressed fundamental reservations: the inflationary gap between the Snake countries and the other Community members was too large to allow a common exchange-rate system. The increase of funds available for intervention would require solid built-in safeguards. A viable monetary system was only conceivable if participants were ready to submit to the rules of the Snake. The German Christian-Democrat opposition spokesmen flatly rejected the plan. The former Bundesbank president, Dr Klasen, warned that Euro-enthusiasm would force Germany to relinquish the relative control it still had over its currency. The Bundesbank once more made it clear that safeguards would have to be built into the system to limit excessive intervention obligations.[17]

But the Chancellor and the President wanted to go ahead. Economic reasoning had to be subordinate to political considerations. The ECU would be at the centre of the new system, both as an embryonic reserve currency and as the pivot of the intervention system. The plan was generally well accepted in France, although subject to criticism. It was rejected almost unanimously in Britain. In Italy the opinion prevailed that high inflation and massive public-sector borrowing requirements would probably make life with the German mark uncomfortable, given the experience with the Snake, and that it would require unpopular stabilization policies. Ireland was in favour under the condition that it obtain considerable financial assistance to meet the difficulties associated with its linking to stronger currencies. The Irish government saw in the plan not only a substantial transfer of resources but also an opportunity to end its monetary union with Britain.

The technical discussions could now proceed: there was agreement about the need for flexibility within the system and for substantial progress towards the coordination of economic policies. A conflict of interest arose about the constraints on strong and on weak currencies, and differences of opinion developed concerning the basket and the complexity of the whole plan. In order to gain acceptance, these technical problems had to be dealt with. The Bundesbank repeatedly criticized the plan because it put pressure on countries with potential surpluses to intervene on an excessive scale in the support of weaker currencies under speculative attack, and recommended that any increase in the amount of credits available for the support of such currencies should be handled with extreme caution.

The Bremen preamble specified that there would be concurrent studies on the action needed to bring the economies of the member countries closer together. The British experts continued to participate very actively in these technical studies but their ambivalent attitudes persuaded the Community partners that there was no real intention to participate in the European Monetary System. The expert committees completed the first phase of their work before the end of September. During a visit by Schmidt and Giscard d'Estaing to the Community headquarters, they announced that something important was happening but remained vague about the details. Again the Bundesbank reiterated its reservations: a massive Fund would fuel inflation and undermine the autonomy of the Bank; the Christian Democratic Union/Christian Social Union (CDU/CSU) opposition claimed that conditions for the creation of a viable system simply did not exist. The British government observed the Franco-German cooperation with suspicion and sarcastic comment.[18]

Months of bilateral and multilateral discussions between experts about the advantages and disadvantages of the different options in the area of parity grid, basket, shifts in emphasis, margins, intervention size and other aspects had taken place. The final phase of the negotiations was even more politicized than the previous ones.

The only driving force had been the commitment by Schmidt and Giscard d'Estaing who dominated the scene. In October a realignment in the Snake forced the Bundesbank to absorb an inflow of DM 10 billion within a short period of time. This gave the Bundesbank president, Dr Emminger, another opportunity to criticize the plan: it was dangerous, unrealistic and untenable.[19]

Schmidt remained undeterred. He was committed to the success of his idea. In France some critics considered that the government only had 'a folding seat beside the command post in the European economy'.[20]

In a long television interview on 16 October 1978, Giscard d'Estaing developed the idea that competition between nations was still fundamental. France had by-passed Britain and within 15 years, if her people showed the necessary determination and if her leaders followed the right policies, the country would achieve the objective of equality with Germany. Europe would then be dominated by two countries of comparable influence. The American economist Herman Kahn had indeed calculated and prognosticated that this would be the case.

The British government remained indifferent and hostile, although Callaghan and his ministers continued to claim that Britain might join if the terms were right. During the following months negotiations about details of the monetary system continued unabated. While these negotiations went on, speculators tested the Snake, forcing the Bundesbank to revalue four times within 18 months.[21]

These events intensified the widespread feeling among experts that the new system was not viable. The discussions about the transfer of resources had been acrimonious from the first meeting on: the less prosperous countries like Italy, Ireland and Britain demanding much more aid than Germany and other countries were willing to grant. In the air of unreality which so often has surrounded the debate about the future of Europe, the discordant squabbling and haggling persisted until the last moment.

At a tense Council meeting in Brussels in December Giscard d'Estaing rejected the demands by Italy and Ireland 'for whom membership seemed to be a question of cash rather than a political will to unite Europe'. Despite substantial loans promised to both countries, the negotiations came to a halt for a 'pause of reflection'. Until the last moment it seemed the plan might never materialize. Finally, after all, on 13 March 1979 the European Monetary System became operational.

11 The EMU House of Cards

News is what the news media say it is. The gathering of information and the production and distribution of newspapers is an expensive business, but it can also be very lucrative. The news agencies and the financial press, owned by or wedded to the corporations who control the financial markets, exert a considerable influence on the views and opinions of the public, carrying with it great potentials for useful information but also great danger of abuse.

Many years ago Oswald Spengler described the power of the press: 'Three weeks of press work and the truth is acknowledged by everybody. Its bases are irrefutable for just as long as money is available to maintain them intact.'

The financial press is in the market for selling and propagating ideas and opinions as well as purely economic information, which gives it the power to set the parameters of ruling opinion among the public and in the world of government. The financial journalist is on safe territory, since his readers often do not know whether he is telling the truth and have no possibility of verifying it; and he knows that tomorrow's news will chase today's. This is not to say that the vast majority of financial journalists do not take their responsibility to the public seriously.

Occasionally, however, the overwhelming desire to serve the hand that feeds them, makes them forget all elementary rules of deontology. One of the most flagrant cases of journalistic abuse in recent years, with consequences that have changed the course of history, was aimed at the Bundesbank.

CONSPIRACY AT THE BUNDESBANK

On 16 September 1992 *The Wall Street Journal* published a news story reporting an interview with Bundesbank president Helmut Schlesinger. Statements attributed to Mr Schlesinger alternated with the reporter's own comments. The sentence 'Market economists expect that the EMS currencies may have to be reshuffled again this time in a massive realignment,' was not attributed and could not possibly have been pronounced by Mr Schlesinger. But the whole article was adroitly construed in such a manner that it could easily be understood as indeed coming from him.

Any other day such an article would have sent tremors through the world's dealing rooms. Timed as it was, it constitutes in retrospect a journalistic coup of the first magnitude. The markets had been in effervescence for several days and were waiting for a signal to launch an attack on the pound with the purpose of forcing it out of the EMS. This was *the* signal. The pound had been under pressure for several weeks and the timing for the assault was right.

Reuters' Frankfurt office, in coordination with the *Journal* flashed the message around the world before the paper appeared in the newsstands. While Europe was asleep the pound traded below its ERM floor in New York and Tokyo.

There had been no realignment in the European monetary system for five years. On 13 September the Italian lira had been devalued by unanimous decision of the EC finance ministers and central bankers, who had expressed confidence that a long period of monetary stability would follow, to be culminated by the creation of a common currency. The EMS was solidly established and had lasted for 13 years. All currencies within the system had been stable since January 1987.

The American bankers had viewed the success of ERM with dismay although they were careful not to voice any strong criticism. Now and then an article would appear in the financial press, expressing doubts about the possibility of a monetary union as long as the policies of the various countries were so divergent. But the financial markets seemed resigned to let it happen, although it would eliminate any prospect of huge profits to be made on intra-European trade, a hope they had not given up.

In June the Danes had rejected the Maastricht Treaty; the financial papers cultivated restlessness, hinting that the lira would probably have to be devalued because of Italy's huge budget deficit and political troubles. Realignments were again on the agenda. France's answer to the Maastricht referendum was uncertain: rejection would cast doubt on the survival of the ERM.

The Anglo-Saxon financial papers worked themselves to fever pitch causing the markets to bristle with effervescent agitation. Currency analysts, market strategists, eminent economists and other experts were on hand to be quoted: unanimously they predicted the suspension or demise of EMS. Day after day the papers kept up the pressure. On 13 September Reuters announced that 'Currency markets have been gambling on an ERM realignment for weeks amid dealers' fears that French voters might kill the Maastricht treaty.'[1]

On 27 August the *Financial Times* had sent up a trial balloon, announcing that a Bundesbank official suggested there was 'potential for realignment'. The Bundesbank immediately issued a denial. Because inflation continued in Italy, the lira seemed like a good target and the speculators started selling lire. They proved to be right. They made huge profits, partly at the expense of the Bundesbank, which spent billions of marks buying up the Italian currency before it was devalued by 7 per cent. The waves of excitation and nervousness generated by these turbulences needed a final impulse that would set in motion the self-reinforcing chain reaction of hope, greed and fear which precedes monetary crises. The foreign-exchange market, bracing for a domino effect, remained impatiently intent on the kind of rumours that turn on the dealers' predatory instinct: they know that speculating against a central bank is a riskless and harmless sport.

They had killed Bretton Woods, they could easily take on the EMS, though they had never seriously tried. If they waited much longer, it would be too late: a common currency would throw most of the dealers on the scrap heap and would dangerously cut profits of the banking system, possibly forever.

On 15 September, the day before the onslaught, *The Financial Times* predicted: 'Only the lira was shaken off this time, but the game is not over yet, however many times British officials may state that the chances of a sterling devaluation are zero.' The pound had for some time been firmly anchored to the mark. John Major hoped to achieve zero inflation by the next election and his policy had strengthened the pound; he had even talked about dethroning the mark as the pivot of European currencies.

LONDON BLITZ

In the morning of 16 September, when the City trading rooms opened, the lid blew off: a wave of frenzied selling hit the pound. One observer noted that the market 'began to smell blood'. It was the beginning of one of the wildest and most frantic days in the history of British finance. The attack on the pound was superbly planned and organized. It was devastating. Market operators felt it would be easy, quick and enormously profitable.

Once more the Bank of England seemed to fall into its own trap. At 8 o'clock, immediately after opening, the Bank started heavy support-buying of the pound. At 10.30 the Bundesbank, and the French and Belgian central banks joined in while the Bank of England announced a minimum lending rate of 12 per cent, the highest since 1985. By 4 pm the Bank's defence of sterling ended for the day. At 6 pm the pound traded below DM2.73. In one day the Bank of England and the other central banks had spent between £15 billion and £20 billion in an effort to shore up sterling. At 7.32 pm, the Treasury admitted defeat: the pound was suspended from the ERM and allowed to float. The following day *The Times* estimated that the cost of the effort to shore up sterling ranged from £2 billion to £10 billion, an estimate that left room for a lot of guessing; but whatever the amount, it was all profit for the speculators. It had been a currency carnage and a proud day for the City.

It produced hyperbolic headlines: 'A Lesson for Europe's Governments', 'A Victory for the Financial Markets', 'Gamblers count proceeds of one-way bet on currency'. *The Independent* exulted: 'Fortunately, the market is much stronger than the Government; it has much more money and much more intelligence.'[2]

Probably the greatest satisfaction besides pocketing the windfall money was that the international banking community had made the politicians look silly. Elsewhere the lira, the peseta and the escudo came under heavy pressure. The lira left the ERM and the peseta was devalued by 5 per cent.

The British politicians blamed the foreigners, mainly the Germans, for their predicament. The Chancellor of the Exchequer, Norman Lamont, blamed the Bundesbank for Britain's humiliation. Chancellor Kohl dismissed Lamont's outburst as 'inappropriate for a minister'. Nobody seemed to know that the whole mess was the consequence of a plot concocted by a few newspapermen in Frankfurt, with the intention of having it immediately blown up by Reuters all over the dealing rooms. It was well planned and if it worked, the financial community would consider it a masterpiece of journalistic cleverness. Reuters has a multi-billion-dollar interest in currency exchange, since it provides most of the foreign-exchange equipment and information.

Mr Schlesinger had gracefully granted an interview to the *Journal* and to the *Handelsblatt*, without suspecting that he would be the victim of a breach of faith. During the conversation he reviewed a broad spectrum of topics and his statements were quoted as such. The interviewer's comment that the 'market economists expected the need for the EMS currencies to be reshuffled' was correctly presented as a comment by the interviewer himself. But the whole article was constructed with deceptive adroitness in such a manner that a superficial and quick reading would lead to the conclusion that these were Mr Schlesinger's words. And this was the way the market operators wanted to read it.

Like most heads of central banks, Mr Schlesinger expressed himself in a most guarded language. In Frankfurt, the Bundesbank protested to Reuters, stating that Mr Schlesinger 'did not say that and it was not what he intended to say'. The message was sent through but the *Journal* never mentioned the denial. A few papers furtively reported it after the crisis was over.

While the bedlam continued in the dealing rooms around the world, Reuters in Frankfurt kept up the pressure, oscillating between the prospect of victory and the fear that the market might be contained. The Reuters man noted with satisfaction that 'The Bundesbank's latest denial that it wants a devaluation of sterling has done nothing to weaken the market's conviction that a further realignment of European Monetary System currencies is on the way.' He called a number of local bankers: all of them were convinced that the pound would be devalued. 'The markets are going to force such a decision,' said the chief economist of the Dresdner Bank. Citibank confirmed: 'Now there's no way out for the pound. It will be devalued.' The following day, the battle over and won, the Reuters man sent frenzied telexes out to the newsrooms:

> Germany's powerful central bank president Helmut Schlesinger came under heavy fire at home and abroad as the European Monetary System unraveled on Thursday. . . . Newspaper editorials both in Germany and abroad blamed Schlesinger for ineptitude. Many called for the Bavarian to resign after 40 years at the Bundesbank. . . . Commentators questioned his motives, wondering whether he schemed to let foreign exchange markets believe that the Bundesbank wanted a broader realignment, or whether incompetence was to blame for 'indiscretions' that let the British pound fall through its EMS floor yesterday. 'There is no possible interpretation of the behaviour of Schlesinger over the past few days other than that he is either a fool or a knave' wrote *The Independent* newspaper in London. . . . 'The sinister interpretation is that Mr Schlesinger was playing another round in the Bundesbank's attempt to force an ERM realignment' *The Independent* wrote. 'The alternative interpretation is . . . simply that Mr Schlesinger is a monetary incompetent unsuited to be put in charge of the Vietnamese dong, let alone the German mark.'[3]

The Reuters man had relayed the Bundesbank's denial and knew very well that Mr Schlesinger's confidence had been betrayed; yet his telexes continued to foment the campaign to be orchestrated by the press. For example:

> Yesterday's crisis was triggered on Tuesday evening by reports of an interview in *Handelsblatt* and the *Wall Street Journal* with Helmut Schlesinger, the Bundesbank president, in which he said the tensions

in the ERM would have been eased more successfully had other currencies realigned with the lira last weekend. With the German central bank apparently uncommitted to defending the pound's parity, sterling sank.[4]

As usual, recriminations and postmortems flew around as to what went wrong, and the search for scapegoats was on. The monetary crisis strained relations between the EC countries. The Chancellor of the Exchequer, Norman Lamont, suggested that 'Frankly, if anyone should resign, it should be the president of the Bundesbank.' He also wanted 'to be satisfied that German policy, which has produced many of the tensions within the exchange rate mechanism is actually going to have some changes and be able to operate within a more stable environment.' The BBC reported that the government was fed up with the Germans.[5]

The press and the politicians were unanimous: the Bundesbank was the culprit. The vindictiveness and factionalism, always present in EC relations, once more sprang to the surface.

The Economist noted with satisfaction that 'Europe's monetary system now faces a test that puts its very survival in doubt.' Conceding that 'Europe's small, open economies cannot work well, let alone as a truly single market, with floating exchange rates,' it predicted that the efforts to create a semi-fixed system might receive more blows. The governments might be tempted to rebuild barriers to international capital flows, but this 'is beyond the wit of governments, and even if it could be done, the cost of international misallocation of resources would be huge'.[6]

Lord Ridley, former Conservative MP, made this comment after the crisis:

Germany and Britain both spent billions of our money in fruitless intervention to save the lira, the pound and other currencies last week. The needless giving of substantial public funds to dealers through fruitless intervention is a disgrace. What have the taxpayers got for the money? Nothing. Intervention cannot work and has never worked in the face of a serious assault upon a currency and should be abandoned. . . . The government should be ashamed of its recent 10 billion ecu loan, part of which it totally wasted when intervening last week. The debt will have to be repaid one day. . . . Mr Major thinks inflation is the chief evil (and so do I). So why should he be cross if the Germans do what he would have done if he had been a German? The Bundesbank, moreover, has a statutory duty to defend the value of the mark. Does he really think they should break the law to suit us?[7]

HIJACKING THE EMS

After the 1992 crisis which had forced the pound out of ERM, it was obvious that 1993 would be another year of argument about the European exchange-rate mechanism and the European Community's hopes of economic and monetary union. Almost everybody in Europe – except the foreign-exchange and derivatives dealers – agrees that currency stability is a necessary aim. In a world of floating exchanges, the banks skim the cream off industry profits, diminishing European competitiveness. Fluctuating currencies in a single market distort competition and make forward planning more difficult, often delaying investment decisions.

The EMS had evolved to a low-inflation zone dominated by Bundesbank policy, to which traditionally inflation-minded countries had gradually adjusted. For years exchange controls made fixed exchange rates compatible with a certain degree of autonomy over monetary policy. The EC authorities had meanwhile eliminated controls on European currencies, but also on the Eurodollar. They would have to discover the impossibility of having simultaneously fixed exchange rates, free capital movements and autonomy over monetary policy. Free capital movements, however, seemed here to stay:

> The reimposition of exchange controls, as suggested in a recent International Monetary Fund report, would be political anathema and a practical impossibility because it would simply mean handing even more power to the markets in New York and Tokyo, monetary sources said. But at the same time, with daily flows across currency markets estimated at some $880 billion, central banks and politicians know that while they might win skirmishes against the speculators they cannot win any prolonged battle.[8]

The September 1992 crisis had left scars in Germany, as more people loudly questioned the advisability of spending huge sums of money to support weak currencies, condemned in advance to devaluation. Chancellor Kohl, however, considered any criticism on the subject as intolerably anti-European.[9]

Early in 1993 the Anglo-Saxon press began to ventilate doubts about the viability of the ERM. In May the peseta and the escudo were devalued with or without reason, except that the speculators had put the two currencies under pressure and maintained turbulence in the market.

In mid-April Reuters announced that the monetary committee of the European Community had issued a report concluding that the

13-year-old currency grid was 'basically sound and all that is needed is better adherence to its rules'. It also stressed the need for changes in the exchange rates to occur well before markets take over the role of policy-making by forcing the devaluation of a currency. The EC officials were confident they could outsmart the speculators by devising a set of secret economic indicators to tip off authorities when a currency was in danger of becoming uncompetitive and thus ripe for devaluation.

If this was the Commission's thinking, it gave evidence of naïveté: the market does not care about indicators or fundamentals. When it feels confident that, for whatever reason, a government will not be able to defend its currency and if it foresees a quick and profitable operation, it will launch an attack. In July 1993 French inflation was at 1.9 per cent, less than half of German inflation. The franc was sound. The market should have attacked the mark; yet it went after the franc.

Ever since the September 1992 crisis the currency markets had been looking for a soft spot and the central banks had been forced several times to intervene heavily. It was obvious that the foreign-exchange markets were tactically braced for a final assault on the ERM. International liquidity, completely divorced from international trade, had exploded. Surveys conducted by the Bank of England, the Federal Reserve Bank and the Bank of Japan suggested that global net turnover was $1 trillion a day – a sum dwarfing the estimated $550 billion of currency reserves held by the industrialized countries.[10]

No amount of bureaucratic self-defence could match such enormous money power. The speculators in the dealing rooms had gradually been joined by institutional investors and by hedge funds, largely unregulated and incorporated in offshore locations, operating primarily by taking highly leveraged speculative positions.

At the centre of this massive financial powerhouse, the Morgan-Rockefeller empire is the only cohesive group effectively controlling an institutionalized global network able to decide when to mount a barrage of money and overwhelm the meagre amounts central banks can summon from their reserves. They can attack in Tokyo, Singapore or New York, while European central bankers are asleep; no coalition of governments has the information and communication power nor the assets to defend itself, let alone to mount a counterattack.

Because of conditions resulting from the reunification, namely an unusually high inflation rate of 4.3 per cent, Germany was maintaining high interest rates; for the first time in 26 years the French discount rate was lower than in Germany. This complete reversal of a decades-old relationship suddenly revealed a basic absurdity at the heart of ERM.

Because of Germany's long history of sound money, a weakening of the mark, despite a higher rate of inflation seemed unthinkable. This sudden anomaly, however, roused French pride and ambitions. The Banque de France expressed its desire to see the franc as an anchor currency within the ERM. Mr Delors, president of the European Commission, 'raised the possibility that the mark could lose its place as the anchor of the European Monetary System to France and the Benelux countries which now have lower interest rates than Germany'.[11]

The moment of glory did not last long. When the French started crowing about their *franc fort* and about its anchor role, Mr Schlesinger, breaking with traditional self-imposed reserve, delivered a calculated insult to the French ministers: 'It takes a long time', he said '– thirty years – to build up the credibility required to back an anchor currency.'

Then a freshman minister entered the scene: Edmond Alphandéry. He announced over the radio that he had taken the initiative of calling his German colleagues to Paris to discuss together the conditions for a reduction of interest rates. 'Europe suffers from too restrictive monetary policies, notably a too restrictive German monetary policy. . . . We are going to talk as equals with the Germans,' Alphandéry said.

Piqued, the Germans cancelled a previously planned meeting. The Bundesbank let it be known that decisions about interest rates are not made by economics ministers but by the central bank.

The inadequacies of the exchange-rate mechanism had allowed the speculators to claim five victims in the past ten months: the pound and the lira had been ejected; the peseta, the escudo and the Irish pound had been devalued. The Commission attributed these devaluations to the new policy of preventing monetary crises by making slight parity alterations; there was nothing wrong with the system as such. The gradual dismantling of capital controls which had held the system together during the 1980s had embrittled the edifice; but as long as it stood there it fed the illusion of solidity.

On 21 July 1993 the Bundesbank met for the last time before the traditional summer pause. Ministers and central bankers were preparing for a relaxed August. The market operators were waiting for a signal that might trigger the attack. The Bundesbank was expected to decide whether or not to lower the discount rate, a decision of little or no consequence to other European countries; but the market jumped on the pretext to launch a demolition assault.

For several months the speculators had successively attacked a number of currencies, forcing the central banks to intervene at huge costs. Every sign indicated that Europe was girding for another currency battle.

J. P. Morgan, in its weekly commentary, observed that 'The Bundesbank's preferred strategy is to use limited foreign exchange intervention,
modest rate cuts and statements in support of the exchange-rate mechanism; the sustained nature of the tensions suggest that these actions may
not be enough.'[12] Such messages coming from Morgan are perceived by
the market operators as watchwords.

STORMING THE BASTILLE

The countdown had started. On Friday, 23 July the Bundesbank and the
Banque de France had to support the franc rate once more. Alphandéry
proudly declared: 'The franc is a sound currency, one of the most stable
in the world. We have the means to combat speculation. We are going to
increase the pressure against it. . . . I am convinced that those who put
in doubt our determination to defend the franc will do so at their
expense.'[13]

As usual, the imminence of crisis was characterized by a firm conviction that all was well. 'France's resolution is beyond doubt,' said President
Mitterrand, 'the EMS must survive.'

Reviewing the September 1992 crisis, the *Financial Times* concluded
on 28 July that 'Currency speculators have rescued EC politicians from
their errors.'

> Huge profits on currency speculation have helped restore bank capital
> at the taxpayer's expense. Being kind to the banks after the excesses of
> the 1980s sounds so shocking to the average citizen that this could not
> have been done by open democratic means. . . . But in a debt-induced
> recession, the restoration of bank capital is a precondition of eco-
> nomic recovery. However unwittingly, the speculators have perpetra-
> ted a most constructive act. It is hard to escape the conclusion that the
> markets have been saving the electorates of Europe from policy, not the
> other way round.

On 29 July the Bundesbank announced that the discount rate would
not be changed. The financial press feigned disappointment. It was in
fact the signal the market-makers had been waiting for: the Bundesbank
had torpedoed the EMS. No time for thinking: sell French francs and
tackle a few other currencies. In Copenhagen, Brussels and Bonn frantic
efforts were made to save the French franc. In Paris Mr Balladur called
an emergency meeting. On 30 July the *Financial Times* predicted a
'bleak summer for the ERM'. The dispute between France and Germany

sparked by Alphandéry's *faux pas* was an open invitation to mount a speculative attack. Cracking the link between the franc and the mark would probably destroy the ERM, the ultimate goal of the Anglo-Saxon international banking community.

The market sensed that the time had come for the decisive attack on the European Monetary System. All must move in the same direction, the whole herd in a stampede against the same central banks. They chose the franc: the Bundesbank, they said, refused to come to the rescue of the French economy; the market would pull France out of its recession.

On 30 July massive sales sent French francs and other ERM currencies considered 'weak' into a tailspin, forcing the central banks to intervene once more. The support was halted for a while as the storm seemed to subside in Europe; but when the New York market opened and put new pressure on the rates, they had to resume their action. 'Torrential flows leave dealers in sunshine,' one paper touted: 'This is a very healthy environment for dealing, but it doesn't occur often,' a dealer said. 'Make hay when the sun shines.'

The Bundesbank had thrown DM60 billion into the turmoil to save the franc; a substantial amount, even for the most powerful European central bank.

DIVIDED WE STAND

The traditional imagery dominating familiar press coverage of monetary crises was back in the headlines. The British and American financial press feigned immense disappointment and indignation: 'German Indifference Puts Franc at Market's Mercy,' shouted the *International Herald Tribune*. Obviously, a slight reduction of the German discount rate permitting an equally slight reduction of French interest rates would have had no impact on the French economy. Long-term interest rates, which are the real concern of commerce and industry, are set in every country by the market and the national bank cartels, not by the central bank; they were lower in Germany than in some other European countries where traditionally less restrictive monetary policies prevailed. Lowering short-term interest rates in France would have had little influence on the French recessionary climate. Moreover, the mythical chain link between the commercial world and the world of finance has become stretchy.

But the Bundesbank's attitude was the only available pretext the speculators could think of, and the market needed a pretext. Market operators are not concerned with theories as they are spelled out in the textbooks, nor with 'fundamentals' or the state of the economy: all they want is *money now.* Sensing imminent action, the forex traders had been staying at their posts while everybody else was on vacation or preparing for it.

The Belgian Prime Minister Dehaene declared: 'The system is based on the principle of solidarity and all the central banks must stick to this principle.' Visibly, the world of politics could not understand why a logically conceived plan, the foundation of the future monetary union, could be intentionally and wilfully attacked and undermined by currency speculators. Nor did the European planners realize that when the EC single-market guidelines made them lift controls on cross-border capital flows, they opened a Pandora's box and exposed themselves to the attacks of a deregulated global currency market led by a cluster of American banks with a century-old tradition of always being in line when it comes to promoting their common interest.

Psychology is a primary factor in dealing with the market; in political circles it is badly lacking. Over the past 25 years monetary crises have followed a routine ritual: when speculators single out a currency considered, with or without reason, ripe for devaluation or revaluation and when they start selling or buying it massively, ministers appear on radio and television making brave and resolute statements about their determination to defend their currency come what may. Just so much pride before the fall.

'The franc is as solid as the Pont-Neuf,' Alphandéry had crowed. Their rhetoric leaves the market unimpressed. When the lights go out in Europe, American dealers are ready, and from there the market moves to the Far East. When the crisis is over, the same ministers, mortified, vexed, grumbling and grimacing, are forced grudgingly to admit defeat, while venting their impotence. Since the beginning of the crisis the Bundesbank had tried to restrain the brunt of the attack by maintaining the franc within its 'obligatory marginal intervention threshold'. According to the EMS rules, when a currency is under attack, the central bank emitting that currency must react by purchasing any amount thrown on the market by the speculators; it must also increase its interest rates. The French did not react, and let the mark float upwards until it reached its ceiling. This put the Bundesbank under the EMS solidarity rule, forcing it to buy the French franc in order to keep it within the limits prescribed by the system.

The French observed how the Bundesbank threw itself into the battle and for a while thought they had won. At the end of the day, the bill for the Bundesbank amounted to DM60 billion, which it had injected into the market in order to save the franc. Enough was enough. A German delegation made a brief trip to Paris in great secret, to discuss a possible common course of action, but without result. The French and Anglo-Saxon press unanimously blamed the Bundesbank.

In Britain there was much *Schadenfreude*. John Major had once observed that the EMU plan had 'all the quaintness of a rain dance and about the same potency'; a statement which had irritated the Commission, seemingly unaware of the primary determinant of British policy in the matter.[14]

The German finance minister decided the time had come for an emergency meeting of both the EC monetary committee and the finance ministers in Brussels.

In the newsrooms monetary crises break the routine; they are welcome and exciting happenings in the life of financial journalists. Attracted by the scent of controversy more than by the arid technical aspect of the debate, which escapes many of them, the newspapers have a great time waging their war of words. The popular press, instead of trying to understand, explain and conciliate, avidly searches for scapegoats abroad and consciously or unconsciously relays much of the information dispensed by Reuters.

The Anglo-Saxon banking community owns the British and American financial press: *The Economist* is a Rothschild fief;[15] *The Financial Times* is a Lazards affiliate and *The Wall Street Journal* is part of the Morgan–Rockefeller empire. Very able and often brilliant journalists provide daily useful general and financial information. They enjoy considerable freedom of expression, provided they stay within set parameters.

Occasionally they will adapt fact and economic theory to the needs of the moment. As everyone who has studied financial history knows, there was a time when financial information was venal. No more. The financial press has become the property and the public-relations arm of the financial community.

Monetary crises bring to the surface nationalistic rancours which one would have expected to be something of the past. Instead of uniting public opinion in the countries under attack against those who cause the crises, they stir things up and put the countries of Europe at loggerheads. 'Paris is a mistress which Bonn can no longer afford to keep,' said *Die Welt*. Commenting on Delors' ambition to replace the D-mark by the franc as the system's anchor currency, *Die Welt am Sonntag* thought this was the symptom of a psychiatric syndrome deriving from the trauma caused by three forced devaluations of the franc in the early 1980s, when he was Mitterrand's finance minister.[16]

In France the press accused the Bundesbank and the Anglo-Saxon speculators in the belief that France and the Anglo-Saxons differ in their economic policies. 'The members of the Bundesbank council are acting like provincial managers,' the *Figaro* thought. 'The EMS is built around the D-mark, those who guard the key currency also have international responsibilities.'[17]

'The war between the international speculators and the central banks is a shock between two cultures,' commented *Le Monde*. 'One is inspired by liberal Anglo-Saxon ideologies, the other by a more continental, dirigiste, ideal.' In a furious lead article the same paper accused Bonn of an economic '*diktat*' and concluded that the time had come to end its ambivalence and state clearly where its allegiance lay. Otherwise 'the current monetary crisis could end in the shipwreck of the European project'.

Le Quotidien thought that the Bonn government had isolated itself: 'It has already lost its friends and tomorrow the consequences of this Prussian obstinacy may seriously jeopardize its own prosperity.' In Italy the *Corriere della Sera* felt that 'The leadership of a system implies that a country is willing and able to take account of the interest of member states and subordinate its national interests to these.' A German observer noted that 'they sometimes confuse our interest with theirs'.[18] Once more the speculators made tempers flare while enjoying the scene. Neither the German government nor the Bundesbank have sought or forced their way into the role of a monetary leader. As the major stable currency bound together in an exchange-rate system with inflation-prone currencies, the anchor role had simply been bestowed upon the D-mark.

SHOWDOWN IN BRUSSELS

On Sunday afternoon, 1 August 1993, the finance ministers of the EC countries trooped into the Borschette centre in Brussels. The flags hung at half-mast: King Baudouin had just died.

On Saturday, after more than six hours of deliberations, central bank and Treasury officials had not been able to reach an agreement. All the available options for easing the crisis had been reviewed. The problems were too important to be left in the hands of the technocrats alone: the outcome would have profound political and economic repercussions and determine the future of the EMS and the more elusive goal of the European Monetary Union.

Germany had called the meeting in the hope that an agreement could be reached before the financial markets opened on Monday. The options available were:

1 a suspension of the ERM for a limited period;
2 the forced exit of several currencies;
3 a devaluation of the franc in return for a reduction of the German interest rate;
4 a widening of the fluctuation bands beyond their current level of 2.25 per cent.

The discussion was tense. About 60 officials from 12 countries, including central bank governors and members of the Commission, attended. It turned out to be a power struggle between the German Finance Minister Waigel and the French minister Alphandéry; both had arrived in Brussels with irreconcilable plans. It was a typical example of the EC gatherings in which political considerations and personal prestige play a more important part than economic or financial considerations. As usual, these meetings are attended by one or more new and totally inexperienced finance ministers who have not had the time or the ability to familiarize themselves with the elementary aspects of the problems.

The Germans made it clear that they could not be expected to provide unlimited support for the French franc, because this would dangerously increase the German money supply and trigger a new inflationary spiral. They suggested that the bands be widened from 2.25 to 6 per cent, which would reduce their obligation to buy currencies under attack. The rule applied already to weak currencies such as the peseta and the escudo.

The French delegation reacted indignantly at the idea that the franc would be reduced to the level of a weak currency. Unthinkable. Rationalizing French ambitions and interests, Alphandéry explained that between the French franc and the other currencies there was no problem. The D-mark was the basic cause of the crisis. So the Germans must continue to support the ERM or leave; technically this seemed to him the most logical solution. The answer was a flat 'no'.

After renewed negotiations, a joint proposal was submitted by the French and German ministers, suggesting that the D-mark leave the ERM. It was a French idea and the French delegation cheered up: the *'franc fort'* had gained the upper hand. In fact, the Germans knew that the ERM needed the mark, whereas the opposite was not true. Waigel had skilfully woven a plot and pulled a fast one: he knew the proposal would be rejected. The Dutch finance minister indeed announced that he wanted to maintain the traditional parity with the D-mark. If the

Germans left the ERM, the Netherlands would follow. Luxembourg and Belgium indicated they would also withdraw. After all, the Bundesbank had for years set the example of a stable and successful monetary policy. The Danes and the Irish joined in: 'if the Germans leave, we leave also'. Schlesinger let it be known that the ERM was an expensive system for Germany: 'We have recently bought weak currencies for more than 60 billion DM, and it is easy to calculate what this costs us when these currencies are exchanged against ecus.'

'Suddenly we were looking at France sitting alone in the ERM with Spain and Portugal,' one participant recalled.[19] Alphandéry fell into the trap he had dug for the D-mark. Waigel had his revenge. He felt that the Banque de France should have increased the discount rate when the speculative attacks gained momentum, instead of demanding that the Bundesbank reduce its own.

Wim Duisenberg, of the Dutch central bank, commented later: 'At the end of the day, the French had to admit that the discount rate is decided upon in one place only: Frankfurt.'[20]

Schlesinger again took some pleasure in rubbing salt in the wound. In remarks clearly directed at French ambitions for the franc, he noted that it takes a mighty long time to build up the credibility needed to establish an anchor currency.[21]

The British Chancellor of the Exchequer, Kenneth Clarke, who was depicted by *The Financial Times* as 'the honest broker between the warring factions in continental Europe,' suggested, in keeping with Britain's traditional policy, that all countries let their currencies float.

The talks then shifted to a possible widening of the fluctuation bands. The Germans suggested that France enlarge the margin to 6 per cent, sweetening the suggestion with the promise to cut their short-term interest rate. The French refused, arguing that this would amount to a devaluation, reducing the franc to a second-rate currency with the peseta and the escudo. Without saying so, the French, swallowing their pride, wanted to prevent a further test by the market.

Sensing defeat and livid at being outmanoeuvred, Alphandéry counterattacked: he demanded that the Dutch break their link with the D-mark. The Dutch retorted that this would make the guilder the strongest currency in the system, exposing it to speculative attacks and forcing it to defend weaker currencies. Such a burden was unbearable for a small country.

Meanwhile Jacques Delors declared on French television that he opposed a general float and recommended once more that the D-mark leave the ERM.[22]

It was 1.45 in the morning; soon the Tokyo exchange would open. A quick decision was indispensable. Around two o'clock the world learned that the European Community had, in a way, saved the European Exchange Rate Mechanism. After considering several variations of wider bands involving various currencies, an agreement was reached on a fluctuation band of 15 per cent for all currencies except the D-mark and the guilder. It was a face-saving agreement giving the franc more room to sink without fracturing the 'mechanism'.

The European Community issued a communiqué announcing the decision: 'This measure of limited duration is in response to speculative movements, which are exceptional in amount as well as in nature.' The negotiations had lasted 12 hours and when the ministers emerged from the meeting room, they looked tired and grim. Visibly downtrodden, the Dutch Finance Minister, Wim Kok, declared: 'It was a very sad day for Europe. The decision to widen the trading parities suffered a difficult birth, and it isn't a pretty child.'

The ERM and its central parity grid had to be preserved, but it was not explained how this would be achieved. The decision imposed by the international banking community constituted one additional dramatic and desperate tactical retreat, a painful blow to the Community's pride. The basic principle of fixed exchange rates had been reduced to a face-saving alibi.

The governments abandoned to the market their prerogative to set their exchange rates. The European dream had run too far ahead of economic and political realities; it had completely discounted and underestimated the power of the international banking community. It was suddenly and brutally fading away.

At half past three Alphandéry declared he had won: 'The franc remains one of the strongest currencies in the world,' he said. 'The destiny of Europe hung in the balance. But France has taken the side of Europe and has saved it. European integration will make further progress.'[23] The French Prime Minister, Edouard Balladur, expressed his satisfaction: 'the franc has preserved its value and the ERM survives'.

The EMS had functioned reasonably well for 13 years and was considered the forerunner and the foundation of the monetary union. Complacency and self-congratulation had taken the upper hand over realistic planning. It had disintegrated after a three-day attack, clearly pointing to its inherent defects.

Traditionally the speculators swap weak currencies for strong ones; this time they reversed their strategy and bet on a devaluation of the

French franc and of the Danish krone, considered among the stablest in the system.

The financial press and the Anglo-Saxon banking fraternity needed a pretext to put an end to the ERM. They could have done so whenever they wanted, considering their superior market power and the system's built-in Achilles' heel due to the monetary amateurism of political decision-makers. The European Monetary System was and remains a fair-weather grand design unable to withstand the hurricanes generated by the international banking community. The defensive intervention instrumentalities available to the European central banks are obviously inadequate to stop an avalanche: all they can do is to hand out windfall profits to the speculators as long as the one-way battle lasts. This time the gaffes of a French minister conveniently provided a detonator.

LUCKY DEALERS LIVE ON CAVIAR AND CHAMPAGNE

As the weary and haggard negotiators returned home, the announcement of the ERM breakdown aroused excitement and jubilation in the dealing rooms. Two decades ago the currency traders had brought down Bretton Woods, but it had taken them three years. This time, with considerably more clout, it had taken three days to liquidate the ERM. Stable rates had stunted the European exchange markets for years, but now the clients would be forced to come back and cover themselves against currency risks. This meant more business, more profits, more power and brightened career prospects. There was the delight of beating the politicians, but counting the chips was even more pleasant. They realized, however, that the days of easy profits from one-way currency bets against the central banks were over. After collecting a huge ransom from the central banks – a source of profits now closed because floating rates put an end to forced intervention – the road was open for collecting ransom from captive private business. They would also have to use the highly sophisticated market-making activities developed over recent years to increase their profits.

The Wall Street Journal reported:

Amid the groans over the virtual demise of Europe's tightly controlled monetary system, one group is trying hard to hide its glee: foreign-exchange dealers. Their career prospects have brightened considerably since the weekend. . . . The widening of the bands within which currencies can fluctuate means greater risk for anyone doing cross-border business in Europe. Companies increasingly will be looking to hedge their exposure. . . . 'A lot of our clients who used to take comfort in the tight ERM bands, now find they have to worry about covering their exposure, and that gives us plenty to do.' . . .

'The collapse of the ERM has been great news for us. . . . Free-floating currencies cause volatility, and that's the key to the derivatives market.'[24]

The ERM, 'a triumph of hope over experience', had for years considerably reduced the banks' profit potential; the monetary union would now probably be dumped. The only danger – very unlikely to materialize – was that the governments impose capital controls. The paper also noted that 'Europe's virtual abandonment of its system of fixed currencies is a humiliating defeat for its political leaders.'[25]

Die Welt thought 'It was a victory for Europe. It withdrew from Utopia and returned to the realm of realities.'[26]

The Financial Times analysed the causes of the crisis: 'France, Belgium and Denmark, all credibly low-inflation countries, were forced last weekend to widen the ERM bands because they could no longer sensibly live with the high level of real interest rates that Germany's structural difficulties were transmitting to Europe.'[27]

Some economists who had thrown their weight on the side of the banking community were delighted. Rüdiger Dornbusch said:

> Only the speculators have the power to force foolish finance ministers back to common sense. . . . We need people like speculators able to send a signal to the politicians: 'Stop, it's silly.' Balladur wanted to show that he could send cows around the moon. The currency speculators bet he could not. Without the speculators the number of unemployed in France would have increased within six months by two hundred thousand.[28]

The former Chancellor of the Exchequer, Lamont, dismissed the Maastricht Treaty as a bit of a fossil. 'The ERM is now dead, and the immediate impact will be for the good since interest rates in Europe will come down and the economy will recover. . . . Reality has caught up with Europe.' He was now only an observer and could say 'we told you so'.[29]

Lamont also made a number of derisive remarks about the ERM: 'It is extraordinary', he said, 'that we have spent so much time constructing this artificial creation and frankly it has gone out of the window. That is the thing I am now free to say as an ex-chancellor but which the finance ministers in Brussels could not say yesterday. Maastricht is now truly dead.' He was rebuked by former Prime Minister Sir Edward Heath: 'That's not diplomatic. You may think it but you don't say it.'

Since August 1993 the currency markets have been relatively quiet. The banks, all of them, are enjoying the increased transactions and new hedging profits. As the pound once ruled the waves, the dollar today rules the airwaves. Finance ministers and central bankers would rather forget what happened because they don't know how to deal with it, while some speculators – not the important ones, who prefer to remain silent – brag about the billions they have forced the central banks to disgorge and the immense profits they so easily made.

Industry and commerce need currency stability, an easier environment for investment and trade. The Anglo-Saxon international banking system does not want fixed rates because much of its revenue comes from foreign exchanges; the United States does not want a single European currency because that would threaten the supremacy of the dollar. The market operators have at their service the most efficient financial press and some of the most prestigious economists. If and when the European Union succeeds one day in establishing a foolproof system that will lead to a monetary union, the profits of the banking system will suddenly shrink, with totally unforeseeable consequences.

THE LONG MARCH

The European dream had run too far ahead of economic and political realities; it had completely discounted and underestimated the power of the global banking community. It had reflected the politico-bureaucratic planning mindset postulating a world that functions according to the wishes of the planners.

Currency fluctuations would gradually taper down through the 'convergence' of economies and the narrowing of the fluctuation bands. In addition, the central banks had a 'secret' threshold at which they were ready to intervene, which would hold off the speculators unable to guess the rules of the game. The basic assumption that the ERM could evolve smoothly into a monetary union before the end of the century and that the Franco-German alliance could move Europe to its political union now looks chancy.

For years it had seemed that Europe's leaders, proud of their economic expertise, had invented a conveyor belt that would unite their nation-states into a single entity. Without realizing it, they were marching Europe up a blind alley. It was evident from the beginning to the experts that the road to a monetary union would be a long and difficult one, paved with setbacks and disappointments.

Between Germany, where the memories of two hyperinflations still haunt the collective memory, and France and Italy, where inflation has been for decades a way of life, plus Britain where the American bankers have restored the primacy of the City, a common economic, monetary and fiscal policy would be long and difficult to bring about. In addition, the assumption that Greece, Italy or Spain would be able within the pre-scribed time to become members of a monetary union anchored to the mark, seem illusory at best .

One of the lessons of these events is that for all their dreams of union, when it comes to making them true, the governments of Europe distrust each other in monetary affairs and are unable to set up a mechanism that will permit them to stand united against the international banking system eager for ever-increasing foreign-exchange profits.

The European governments, prodded by the Commission, are going ahead with their plans for a monetary union by the end of the century. The Economic Affairs Commissioner Henning Christophersen said in an interview: 'I don't think we can go back to narrow bands unless it is underpinned by a clear political determination to coordinate economic policies much better.' As for the possibility for a majority of countries to adopt a single currency by 1997: 'I will not completely reject that possibi-lity, but it is clear that it can only be done if there is a clear change in the present economic cycle. I don't believe you will have a majority of mem-ber states meeting the Maastricht criteria if we are going to have another two or three years of low or no growth.'

The Belgian Finance Minister Maystadt seems to have a more realistic appraisal of the situation:

> We can draw lessons from the last crisis, which was not caused by fun-damental economic elements but by speculation against the EMS itself. I tell myself that it must be possible to find the means so that it is no longer so easy for speculators to upset the system.

Recalling that the EC's directive on free movement of capital allowed member states to invoke a 'safeguard clause', Maystadt said: 'I wonder if it is absurd to think the EMS itself could also resort to a safeguard clause by having a means of defence against speculation. . . . It would be fool-ish to narrow the divergence margins without having devised defensive weapons.'[30]

In the last issue of 1993, *The Economist* observed that all the European currencies had clambered back to within $2\frac{1}{4}$ per cent of their central rates against the D-mark. A formal return to an ERM of narrow bands, however, was unlikely:

> Such an attempt would fail in any case: the markets would test central
> banks' willingness to defend the bands. With their economies in recession, the banks would have no stomach for the fight. Nor should they.[31]

12 Banking in Wonderland

In the chequered history of banking, the emergence of the Eurodollar will remain as *the* major development since the appearance of banknotes. This banking revolution has hardly transformed the basic functions of the overwhelming majority of Community banks, even when they have nationwide networks. They have simply added departments to handle Eurocurrency transactions. These institutions are still populated by *routiniers*; very few belong to the gambling type of creative entrepreneurs. Said one of Europe's major bankers: 'Deposit banking is, in a way, a boring profession because it pays to be cautious.'[1]

These bankers continue to play an indispensable role. Like the old-time goldsmith-bankers, they attract money deposits from the public and recycle these deposits to grant loans to individuals and corporations. They provide the infrastructure for the day-to-day payments and transfers without which our economy would grind to a halt. These banks are subject to the rules and regulations of the country in which they operate: adequate capital, minimum reserve requirements, bank cartel rates and so on.

Engaged in traditional banking, using constantly improving technology, such institutions are generally very well managed. In Europe bank failures are rare and, with very few exceptions, such as Herstatt and a few others in recent years, the government or the banking community will intervene to protect depositors and other creditors. In the United States bank failures are commonplace. Dozens of banks, generally small, disappear every year; in 1984 there were 79 bank failures, the highest figure for nearly 50 years. There was a systemic crisis in the whole Ohio state banking system and many farm banks were pushed to the brink of insolvency. Continental Illinois had to be rescued by the government before being taken over by the Bank of America.

In the 1980s American taxpayers had to stump up over $150 billion when hundreds of savings banks and loan associations went bankrupt. This revived an old American problem: if a government promises to protect depositors against bank failures, the absence of discipline becomes increasingly dangerous as the bank approaches insolvency. Once they have lost their capital, the owners of the bank have little to lose by chancing anything on a last desperate throw.

After World War II the large American banks had been run on traditional lines by very conservative, middling people. Many had got their fingers burnt during the 1930s; public opinion blamed the Depression on Wall Street and on the banks in general. Chastened by their past mistakes, they had no desire to repeat the experience.

With the advent of the Eurodollar a new generation of American bankers rose to prominence, avid to take advantage of the political and economic supremacy of the United States and to develop this new, mysterious and revolutionary parallel money market growing up in London and served to them on a silver platter by Soviet-owned banks.

A BANKER'S PARADISE

The activities of the banks described in this chapter have in common with the traditional national banking system the supreme value of agreements. Eurobankers differ in that they put the power of trust above the force of law. Most banks involved in the Eurodollar market have maintained their traditional operations; the new departments operate side by side but separately. These departments and the new banks, created exclusively to operate in the Eurodollar market, have evolved out of the modest clandestine dollar transactions in Paris in the 1950s to become a 24-hour-a-day integrated global money market with activities shifting from one time zone to the next as one continent wakes up and the other goes to bed.

The Eurodollar owes its fabulous growth to the City. London, the world's largest offshore banking centre, in 1983 averaged one foreign bank opening every two weeks. A foreign banker wishing to set up an office starts with a visit to the Bank of England. He will be escorted through vaulted corridors by a pink-coated attendant – called a 'gatekeeper' – and will meet with the head of banking supervision. To become a licensed banker he fills out a form containing 20 basic questions, gives a detailed statement of accounts and explains his intentions. The Bank of England then agrees with the newcomer on an opening date, which is seldom more than three months ahead.

Once established, he will be allowed to transfer a high proportion of his profits to holding companies elsewhere and set the rest of his expenses against the remainder. By contrast, in most other countries, it takes long discussions with inspectors and auditors, heaps of paper and many months of waiting. The Bank of England deliberately exercises its powers with restraint, taking the view that the foreign banks operating in London are supervised by the authorities of their own countries. As soon as it is established the new bank can start operations: no local capital is needed, no minimum reserves are required, no limits are set on the volume of lending and the interest rates are freely decided by the banks. This is truly banking in wonderland.

Clustered within the square mile, these banks have discovered and invented a number of fabulous instruments to create money out of thin air: interbank lending is probably the most important and profitable, a technique which has become the mainstay of the Eurodollar market and has fuelled the superabundance of liquidity, far beyond the requirements of commerce and industry.

This is a clubby arrangement between 'Names'. The banks lend to each other at the Libor rate – London Inter Bank Offered Rate – creating money in the process, which enables them to grant loans to corporations, governments, government agencies and other customers. By taking deposits from other banks, they can increase liquidity quickly and indefinitely.

Economic growth requires finance; but when the superabundance of liquidity exceeds by far the needs of commerce and industry, the only way to put it to use is to trade money for money or other liquid assets.

The exponential growth of the Euromarket has been supported by low-cost information processing through a constantly improved and refined communications technology. Globalization, deregulation and technical innovation have completely transformed the way the banks operating in the international markets carry out their functions. Ever since its inception, the extraordinary inventiveness of the financial operators, adding sophistication to power, has been constantly creating new financial instruments, new markets and new institutions, in part to avoid taxes and administrative controls. Driven by the need to bid for business in a fiercely competitive environment, they have ingeniously created ways to circumvent official restrictions, pouring through every gap as soon as it was noticed, until they established a new and totally independent closed-circuit money market where technology is moving so fast that what is new today is out-of-date tomorrow.

Here inventiveness and ingenuity reign supreme: so do laissez-faire, competition, wheeling and dealing, largely divorced from the world economy, a permanent global casino occasionally on the verge of hysteria. International banking has become a high-reward and high-pressure profession, involving dazzling financial sophistication, energy and risk-taking. Here the prudent tightrope exercise of traditional banking becomes a high-wire act; over and again an imaginative brain will discover a new instrument and try to lure new customers into the game. In *Euromoney* jargon, the participants are called 'players'.

The Euromarket revolutionized the nature of banking; by unifying national financial markets, it established a single global money market. The creation of the cooperative society SWIFT (Society for Worldwide Interbank Financial Telecommunication) – located in Belgium – in the early 1970s has been another milestone. A computer-based message-switching network providing a private global communications service between members, it carries hundreds of thousands of payment messages a day at the cost of a few pence or cents.

Transactions take place in a private currency which is not money but a *claim* on money. Eurodollars are not legal tender – or lawful money – in any country. They must be exchanged for a national currency to be accepted as a means of payment. Paul Samuelson's observation that 'Since the beginning of recorded history, governments have had constitutional authority over money,' must now be qualified.[2]

The concept of an international private currency has come to be accepted as a *fait accompli* by all national authorities, although it constitutes a negation of secular economic doctrine.

As late as 1967, this century's greatest financial wizard, who knew all the ins and outs of money, who had manipulated it and performed more tricks than anybody else, stated:

> For this reason there is no such thing as international currency. It is unlikely that it will ever come into being. International money would have to be granted the status of legal tender in all countries in which it circulates. In all these countries it would have to be possible to settle every state and private obligation in this currency. Any institution controlling this currency irrespective of whether it is a bank or a government department would dominate the world – an unthinkable situation. Currency is the most nationalistic factor in political life. Every central bank responsible for issuing it is dependent on the government of the country by whose laws it was instituted, and which makes its notes legal tender in the country's home territory. The granting of credit is unthinkable without a central bank. No central bank can be allowed to act against the government of the country. . . . No state will surrender so much of its sovereignty that its partners or competitors are given the power to prescribe its economic and financial policies.[3]

This must have been the reassuring certitude soothing the minds of European central bankers in the early 1960s, as they reigned over their national domains from their impressive fortresses. But certitude is not the test of certainty.

Until then, the central bankers held the world of international finance together by the power they derived from the reserves they controlled and by exerting subtle pressure when and where they felt the need. The role of public institutions is to ensure that private financial institutions create credit in the amounts and for the purposes desired. In Europe, all countries regulated bank deposit rates and allowed their banks to reduce interest-rate competition by fixing rates in cartel.

Starting in the 1960s, when central bankers still administered their national finances, holding the purse strings, a few American banks operating from London, while continuing to provide traditional banking services to their clients on the Continent, surreptitiously began to grant Eurodollar loans. By national law, it was an act of poaching. For the Eurobanks, operations that were illegal nationally became possible internationally because not expressly prohibited or even noticed. Exploiting the loopholes in the law, often abetted by sympathetic or absent regulators, the Eurodollar market expanded by leaps and bounds.

Eurodollars and United States dollars are closely linked, like central bank money and credits. Yet, they are not identical. The banks providing loans to their clients on the Continent were acting in fact as predators-at-large, doing tricks with money under the unsuspecting central bankers' noses. The Eurodollars were provided by the London-based branches of American banks, with the blessing of the Bank of England. As a precautionary measure, however, British companies were forbidden access to the Eurodollar market.

A new type of international currency transcending national boundaries and scorning supervision was now being smuggled into the Continent. It escaped national rules and regulations; it was not subject to minimum reserve requirements nor capital-to-assets ratios. The banks could grant loans at below-cartel rates. There was no safety net in case of trouble, but this seemed immaterial. In a national market, a central bank seeks to ensure controlled growth and stands by to prevent a sudden contraction of credit. In the Eurodollar market, the amount of credit creation was limited only by the clients' demands.

Thus the European economy faced the paradoxical situation where the creation of international liquidity was freely permitted in the form of Eurodollars in those very regimes where the expansion of domestic money was strictly and severely controlled.

The Eurodollar is an interest-bearing deposit; it remains within the banking system. Not being legal tender, only when the end-user exchanges it against a national currency can it be used to effect payments.

The new stateless currency brought into existence a new generation of pioneering and adventurous bankers, opening new frontiers, exploring unknown territories, unravelling the complex and mysterious mechanisms of international finance, known only to the initiated, the practitioners of the art, members of the club.

International money operates within time zones, not within national boundaries. National finance has national rules, global finance has global rules. By linking national financial markets, the Eurobankers have created a single global money market. They are capable of mastering the most arcane legal niceties to get around rules and regulations, while preserving a high concern for apparent law-abiding respectability in the face of governments.

Mutual confidence is the most valuable asset in the Eurocurrency market. Since the loans are unsecured, they are only granted to 'Names', to corporations, governments or government agencies whose ability to repay seems beyond doubt. Except during periods of crisis, after a bankruptcy within the system, or when the market suddenly breaks down, funds in unlimited quantities are globally available, at a price. This laissez-faire unsupervised atmosphere has opened up enormous new opportunities to wheel and deal on a global scale.

The nature of Eurodollar financing necessarily favoured corporations of known standing, able to absorb large loans. These loans can be made quickly and easily, often by telephone, to be confirmed later in writing, involving little or no inquiry as to the purpose of the loan. Compared with borrowing in national markets, borrowing in Eurodollars can be done without the customary formalities and at relatively low cost. The Euromarket is remarkable for its flexibility, adaptability and resilience, resulting in part from the absence of official regulation. The Eurodollar is the perfect instrument for the perpetuation of John Pierpont Morgan's concept of centralization of industry: it is only available to large corporations, and, as such, discriminatory. It allowed American companies to eliminate many smaller European competitors.

From the beginning, a handful of very large banks dominated the market. They still do. They are the pillars of the Morgan–Rockefeller empire: Citibank, Chase Manhattan, Morgan Guaranty, Bankers Trust; Manufacturers Hanover merged with Chemical in 1991. Chase Manhattan merged with Chemical in 1995 to become the largest bank in the United States. For over a century they have been the core of American international banking and as such the mainstay of American investment abroad.

In the 1930s nine American banks had foreign branches. In 1950 the seven American banks operating abroad had 95 offices. With the exception of the Roosevelt era, the same institutions have constituted the inner circle of the politico-financial-economic power of the United States.

THE EUROBANKER

Walter Wriston, chairman of Citibank, who epitomizes the Eurobanker, wrote:

> The clash between governmental economic planning and personal liberty is inevitable because, in the end, governmental allocation of either economic or intellectual resources requires the use of force. . . . The hand of government touches every aspect of human productivity. It is not only wasteful, but serves to destroy incentive and to discourage ingenuity. . . . Their desire to control the international financial markets as they control so many national financial markets is, however, a vain wish.[4]

Wriston scorned politicians and bureaucrats 'whose business in life it is to regulate, and who still do not understand that the world has become one huge international market place'.[5]

Regulation was his bogey. In the spirit of John Pierpont Morgan, no one openly emphasized with the same forcefulness the primacy of individual interests over collective obligations. Both domestically and internationally he was the trailblazer for new devices thought up to sidestep government regulations. He joined First National City Bank in 1946 as a $2800 auditor and rose steadily to the top to become chairman of Citibank. His major brainchild was the negotiable certificate of deposit – the CD – which was to allow banks to circumvent Federal Reserve Board regulations regarding the payment of interest on cheque accounts. Before the regulators had time to find out whether it was legal, the CD was a fact of life. He also pioneered the recycling of petrodollars.

In pursuit of its declared ambition to be the most powerful bank in the world, Citicorp has thrown satellites into orbit. In 1990 the company employed about 100 000 people. Banker of the year, Wriston was asked by *Euromoney* to write an editorial on the occasion of its tenth anniversary. Excerpts are:

> Eurocurrency markets are completely regulated by national monetary policies. They are primarily markets for intermediation rather than

credit creation. . . . The Eurocurrency markets have not accentuated exchange rate fluctuations. . . . Nor is there any evidence that the world markets have worsened world inflation.[6]

He paraphrased in his own terms Walter Bagehot's statement that a well-managed bank needs no capital but that no amount of capital can save an ill-managed one:

> The capital is a very interesting concept, and defined in all kinds of ways. At the end of the day, the definition of adequate capital is supplied by the marketplace, and the marketplace believes that you have enough or you don't.[7]

For a decade Wriston dominated world banking; he was the recognized master and beacon for the rest of the community. He organized the recycling of OPEC surpluses through massive lending to developing countries whose external payments were falling into deficit as a result of the oil price increases. For a while it was obvious that the banks knew much more about money than hidebound and uninventive bureaucracies, unable to circumscribe rapidly an entirely new problem which taxed their imagination.

Mutual congratulation and self-conceit permeated the banking community. Transforming volatile short-term OPEC deposits into loans to poor countries, with maturities extending over years, obviously involved risks for the banks. Their obsession with short-term profits prevented them from directing attention to the ability and capacity of the borrowers to pay interest and reimburse the capital. Moreover, much of the money, instead of being put to use for productive purposes to enhance export competitiveness, disappeared into numbered accounts.

When this led Citibank and the rest of the large American banks into trouble, Wriston spearheaded the lobbying for help from governments and official organizations to have the loans rolled over or replaced. One of his smartest coups resulted in having a number of governments and international organizations lend money to Latin American countries so they could pay interest to the American banks. A Mexican official explained:

> The problem was that after some time the ones who were lending us even these modest amounts of 'new money' were no longer banks but governments. The banks didn't deliver their share. And after two or three years of this strategy, which was later called the Baker Plan, the

governments started realizing they didn't like it. Public money was going into debtor countries to pay commercial banks.[8]

When he joined the bank in 1946, the assets were $4 billion and the overseas division was a relatively minor operation. When he left at the end of 1982, Citibank had over 2000 branches dotted around the globe and $120 billion in assets.

Foreign exchange became its main source of profits. In one year, between 1977 and 1978, Citibank recorded a 700 per cent increase in profits from foreign-exchange trading: from $13 million to $105 million. During the same period J. P. Morgan's foreign-exchange income expanded only from $40 million to $56 million.[9]

The Morgan–Rockefeller empire is the cornerstone of the Euromarket, the originator and organizer of new concepts that made it grow; it has been in the forefront of all the monetary winds and speculative orgies that have blown through the exchanges since its inception.

In 1979 its share of the total Eurocurrency market was estimated at 22.5 per cent. Citicorp came first with 9.08, followed by Chase Manhattan with 5.5 and Morgan Guaranty with 4.93. Bankers Trust had 1.9 per cent and Manufacturers Hanover Trust 1.08.[10]

Only seven competitors had more than 2 per cent of the market. The rest was divided between hundreds of banks all over the globe. Ten years later its share was reduced to about 13 per cent, for the reason that a growing number of banks had jumped on the bandwagon. The recognized leader of the Euromarket now had powerful allies in its battle for supremacy in the struggle for world financial domination.

When Wriston retired, his star had begun to fade:

> The coup de grace symbolically took place at the time when John Reed, the young and rather brash new chairman of Citicorp, decided to seize the initiative and separate himself from the old regime. In technical banking jargon, in one fell swoop he 'provisioned', or reserved, $3 billion against Citibank's Third World debt, 20 per cent of the total. That meant an enormous 'hit' to the bank's bottom line, and it ended the year with a loss unprecedented in American banking.[11]

Under Wriston, Citibank had by far overtaken Chase in size and importance. David Rockefeller, chairman of Chase, although part of the same empire, was his most visible rival. Rockefeller considered himself the senior statesman of the American banking establishment, spending much time as roving ambassador, meeting with heads of state, at home with the Shah, with Latin American generals, with Communist leaders.

MAXI-PROFITS THOUGH MINI-TAXES

Small firms and the self-employed practise tax evasion, which is reprehensible and illegal; sophisticated corporations practise tax avoidance, which is considered acceptable and quite honourable. Tax avoidance courses in some universities are several years ahead of foreseeable tax laws. As institutions whose profits depend to a large extent on the ability to lawfully avoid rules and regulations limiting profit maximization, these corporations have upgraded tax avoidance into a science and an art. Citibank became involved in a widely publicized lawsuit when a scrupulous employee reported to the head office violations of European tax and foreign-exchange-regulation laws. The man had been fired.[12]

In the late 1960s and early 1970s many banks set up shell branches in the Caribbean tax havens. A shell branch is not a bank but a contrivance to get around bank regulations and tax laws.

The Eurodollar market has survived a number of scares and crises. The Herstatt failure in June 1974, which involved a default on obligations in the foreign-exchange markets as a result of massive speculative losses, immediately transformed separate domestic banking difficulties in different countries into an international banking crisis. When such a crisis erupts, fear suddenly replaces gambling instinct and greed. During the following summer the crisis took on a frightening shape. The technique of interbank dealing in deposits had revolutionized banking around the world. Having invented it, the banks discovered how it could fall apart.

International finance today is overwhelmingly a private system, involving only marginal official involvement. The tumultuous transition from a government-controlled monetary system to a market-dominated system provided, for several years, newspaper headlines and headaches for European finance ministers and central bankers. The successive monetary crises, from the late 1960s to July 1993, were the visible manifestations of the struggle between governments and private banks for control over international finance. The closing of the United States gold window in August 1971, the manoeuvres around the Smithsonian Agreement, and the second devaluation of the dollar were stations on the road from the Bretton Woods fixed-rate system to a regime of floating rates.

Europe tried to create a regional zone of currency stability, but the combined power of the American Administration and of the international banking community relegated the dream to limbo. At the climax of each crisis, the press and television showed the European finance ministers' grim faces and the frantic activity in the dealing rooms. The men in the boardrooms where the strategy and the tactics against governments were elaborated, neither talked nor took the rostrum. A few midget speculators attracted undeserved attention.

In a world of floating exchanges, the international banking community, under the leadership of the Morgan–Rockefeller empire, has supreme control of world finance, collecting a levy on international transactions, skimming the cream off commerce and industry, and playing a $1 trillion-dollar-a-day game for fun and profit. It conforms with good grace to the inspectorate and the regulations of the national authorities, proceeding via endless compromise with tax men and regulatory bodies. The game has been won; the predatory old ways have been abandoned or disguised.

The Euromarket continues to grow and flourish because there is no authority to breathe down its neck. It simply runs itself. European governments have little ground for vexation; the Italian, French, Belgian and British governments queued up in the 1950s at the Eurodollar's baptismal fonts and brought the market into existence.

Since then, many large and medium-sized European banks have copied the idea, climbed on the bandwagon and broken out of the national-cartel straitjacket to engage in international debt, equity and derivatives operations. Competing for market shares as syndicate loan arrangers and lead managers, they have gone global, bringing down barriers and opening up markets, tapping potential investors from Asia to the Middle East and Latin America. Some European governments and institutions have become their most regular customers.

And so, more than ever before, money makes the world go round; everyone, investor, borrower and banker trying to make the best of it.

13 The Global Money Game

The foreign-exchange market has developed within less than three decades from a conservative traditional trade-based banking operation to a self-sustaining exponentially growing and venturesome meeting place for intrepid traders. The players are bonded by a community of interests: keep the game going.

Currency speculation is said to be a zero-sum game: the cumulative profits equal the cumulative losses. However, since its incipience in the late 1960s the participants seem to have accumulated astronomical sums of money. The market operates largely outside the real economy in a world all of its own. For the overwhelming part of their activities, the foreign-exchange markets serve no useful purpose for world commerce; they have departed from their traditional role of serving international trade and have become preoccupied predominantly with speculative transactions.

In 1979 the estimated combined market share of the Morgan–Rockefeller banks was about 22 per cent. In 1986 the group's share of the foreign currency market was about 17 per cent. They *are* the market, both as major providers of liquidity in the interbank market and as market-makers.

In the world of foreign exchange, a delicate but impenetrable curtain is being drawn between the market-makers – Citibank invariably at the top – and those who are satisfied with a more or less secure niche which they try to expand and consolidate. The market-makers constitute the inner circle of the huge dealing operations where the hardest prices in the world are to be found. Only the biggest and bravest spot teams can afford to quote both sides of the market when the dollar whiplashes four or five cents up and down within the same day.

The operations are overwhelmingly interbank transactions, like a single artificial brain covering the earth, coupled with a nerve centre incessantly receiving innumerable stimuli, like a seismograph hypersensitive to all types of developments. The merest rumour – an assassination or a violent volcano eruption – can inject volatility in the quietest of days. For years foreign-exchange-market dealing was driven by relatively predictable patterns of trade flows; since the late 1960s, by huge and often unpredictable capital flows. Until that time currency dealing was a negligible activity in the banking community.

Ever since, until July 1993, when the European Monetary System crumbled after a three-day attack by the currency speculators, monetary crises have regularly made headlines. On each occasion the currency markets were like a gambling house with the odds rigged in favour of the gamblers rather than the house. The press presented these currency gyrations as 'speculation against the dollar'. In fact, the dollar was used to speculate against the European central banks. The banking community, spearheaded by the large American banks with branches all over the world, dumped on the European central banks billions of dollars created in the interbank market. Central banks were forced by international agreement to mop them up and exchange them for their lawful currencies. They lost billions in the process and apparently never learned that intervention only serves to enrich the speculators.

Now that currencies are floating, the era of one-way risk-taking is over. Instead of playing against central banks, every single trader faces another professional in a battle of wits.

The international banks' corporate exchange departments, once a marginal back-room operation conducted by a few specialists, have moved to become a prime source of bank earnings. They can also spell disaster. Since every currency transaction involves a sale and a purchase, one man's gain is another man's loss. Large banks can generally absorb the results of their errors, although there have been exceptions, such as Continental Illinois. Small banks, such as Herstatt, could not and were wiped out. Many losses resulted from allowing dealers to attempt covering a small initial loss by entering into a series of larger transactions on a double-or-quits basis. In 1980 trading in the foreign-exchange market averaged $75 billion a day. By 1986 daily turnover had increased to $200 billion and had become overwhelmingly speculative. In 1993 the share of trade-based transactions was reduced to about 1 per cent. A market traditionally serving trade and investment had become a global money game.

The banks, having created billions of dollars for which there was no legitimate demand in the economy and no commercial use, and burdened with costly global branch networks, had to look elsewhere for profits. The services these banks used to provide are no longer in demand and lending is no longer considered an attractive business in its own right. Disintermediation in financial services has prompted a frantic search for survival strategies. The direct financing of corporations has been largely replaced by a more sophisticated role in the distribution of securities to investors worldwide. Banks have replaced their traditional income from loans by a more controversial activity. From lenders they became traders in currencies, securities, swaps, and other derivatives, in a very volatile game.

Sophisticated computer technology, developed and constantly refined, whisks billions in an eye's blink from one continent to another. Innumerable news flashes carry information, rumours and hunches across boundaries in seconds. Interpreting the information has become more basic than receiving it quickly. The name of the game is to anticipate market reaction to each news item appearing on the screen and to guess what everybody else is going to do. Markets are the net result of what people think likely to occur, not the result of events but human reactions to these events by traders around the world. Day after day the market sets the exchange rates. If there is an academic or political judgment that a currency is undervalued or overvalued, the judgment will be wrong unless and until the market proves it right. Largely divorced from the real economy, the banking community can flourish while industry and commerce suffer a prolonged recession.

The real economy needs stability; international banking thrives on volatility. For many years the City was an island of prosperity amidst a stagnating national economy. This pattern has now extended to the European continent; the disparity between the flourishing financial community and the rest of the economy has increased year after year. The major stock markets all over Europe reach all-time highs while every day factories close down or dump redundant workers from their payrolls on to the welfare state wrestling with perennial deficits and accumulated debts.

Tens of thousands of young men and women, riveted to their Reuters or Quotron terminals, their telex and computerized telephone systems, spend their working days watching simultaneously several screens while talking on several phones at once. The currency trader must absorb the incoming messages and anticipate which change in the news or in the mood of the market will prevail in bending the mass psychology of his counterparts. He must 'take a view', outwit the crowd and try to pass the depreciating currency on to the fellow at the other end of the line. He knows that every time he sells, some other professional dealer must buy.

Forecasting is difficult in any market, but in the case of foreign exchange, where money itself is the commodity, the determinants influencing price are more complex and elusive than in any other area. Currency analysis is more an art than a science, a financial chess game involving a subjective evaluation of conflicting data, the ability to sense the mood and the psychology of the market and the extent to which expectations of future events are discounted.

Dealers are not a bunch of scholarly PhDs searching through statistical evidence for proof that a certain currency rate is becoming over- or undervalued, thereby triggering a decision to buy or sell. Economic insight is irrelevant: what counts is to guess better than the crowd what direction the market will take and bet on that trend. Foreign traders have been taught by harsh experience that betting on the longer-term fundamentals is a sure way to get fired. They focus primarily on short-run developments. The future to them is no more than a few minutes or seconds away.

Today's typical money trader is in his or her late twenties or early thirties, with a good sixth-form or university/high-school or college education. In a market dominated by greed and apprehension, they must be possessed by the nagging cupidity of the gambler, capable of making their own decisions, and at the same time be constantly aware of the fact that dealing-room discipline is paramount. The market will bury undisciplined traders. They may never have seen or touched a Dutch guilder or a D-mark; to them they are numbers on a screen that link them with other dealing rooms around the world.

Banks run different risks in different degrees; some manage risk better than others. The head traders of dealing rooms must have a good idea of the general picture of the market and of the prevailing risks; they must adjust their overall exposure in each market and determine how much rope to give to the individual traders, while leaving each of them a good dose of autonomy in his or her particular area. They keep the traders advised on the overall picture and let them know if and when they are out of line.

Every dealing room has its own ambience and climate, its history and sensitivities; a highly coordinated group sets the parameters within which the individual dealer can make risk-decisions, each participant being simultaneously dispenser and receptacle of information. Every dealer has his or her own pattern of behaviour acquired by trial and error, enabling them to concentrate on guessing the trend. Losses early in the career may reduce their confidence when pulling the trigger at the next opportunity.

The ghost hovering over the currency trader is the ghost of Nathan Mayer Rothschild who was the first to know the outcome of the battle of Waterloo and made a fortune at the expense of everybody else. Fast couriers and homing pigeons have been replaced by satellites and fibre-optic cable blinking an unrelenting flow of messages; any scoop is available simultaneously to all dealers in the time zone and in some of the City's largest dealing rooms the lights never go out.

The same phenomenon is evaluated in different ways depending on the evaluator's knowledge and ego-defence. The market is irrational and decisions are seldom made on logical thinking; its verdicts are derived from a cascade of anticipations by market-makers followed by the rest of the crowd. This becomes particularly evident when a monetary crisis erupts; then the mass of dealers attacks central banks and the market reacts before the news that makes it move is known and understood by government officials.

Dealers are rated according to their ability to read the market, by the yields they get and the profits they realize. Risk-taking must be balanced with prudence, greed with patience. Keeping one eye on the screen and the other on the news services, they perform a daily mental juggling act, trying to beat the gun and outwit the crowd. They must be aware of what is happening outside their own narrow market; in the successful dealing rooms individuals work together as a team, every dealer taking on the collective wisdom of the moment.

Traders are culled from university or off the street. Young traders are weaned carefully. The newcomers may spend about a year working with a senior manager, then rotate within the various product areas before being given a chance to prove themselves. They must above all shed their Pavlovian conditioning. During this period macro-economic researchers, technical analysts and sales staff will dispense advice. When the time comes, a dealer may be allocated a position limit; experience and profitability will gradually determine how much each gets.

A DAY IN THE LIFE OF A CURRENCY DEALER

When a London dealer opens up in the morning he does not start dealing at the previous day's closing prices but works on rates in the Far Eastern markets. Nearly all foreign-exchange deals take the form of purchases or sales of one currency against the dollar.

During the night the trading room has been inundated by information dispersed through the screen-based global news networks. His job is to respond to this never-ending stream of fresh information, tackle it and separate the important from the trivial. Buy? Buy what, how much and at what price? Sell? Same questions. What will the market do? Will it buy or sell? He thinks through the arguments for an increase of a given currency and the arguments for a decrease. Then he must decide whether to go 'long' or 'short' in dollars against the currency he trades. He keeps staring at his computer screen, monitoring the dollar second by second, which will give him the mood of the market. Most important is to keep his cool.

The fact that he was good yesterday does not guarantee that he will be good tomorrow. A serious and repeated mistake or a big loss through incompetence may put his job and his family's security on the razor's edge. The nerves strained by uncertainty in a never-ending stream of fresh data, he must evaluate the relative importance of each news item.

A sudden rumour in the market, a statement made by a finance minister or a central banker, can distort rates on a scale that defies all rational analysis and incite the trader to an urgent rush to cover positions. The market thrives on hints, greed and fear, and the dollar is in the thick of it, the currency against which all others are measured. He must decide 'where the sheep will go and get there a little sooner'. His bank's performance ultimately rests on his competitive skill and that of the other traders. Between the devil and the deep blue sea, with the constant prospect of a windfall killing, stress is his permanent companion. Said one dealer:

> The most difficult time is when it's quiet. People stare at their screens and become increasingly nervous. Then they begin to persuade themselves that they have missed out on some crucial piece of information that everyone else knows about. A kind of neurosis of fear sets in.[1]

Doctors have observed that dealers will perform at maximum efficiency when mental stress reaches its climax. After a while, they tend to become more easily irritable, to take to the bottle and smoke too much, to spend sleepless nights and to lose interest in any activity besides dealing. Here each of them has to find his own balance and temporary escape. Many of them have few interests outside the office. Because of the intense competition, happiness is money and the glamour of the 'big deal'. This then becomes their finest hour.

Despite the piles of money they make, dealers are not necessarily a happy and satisfied bunch. In June 1995 a senior trader of Salomon Brothers abruptly resigned. It was not quite clear whether he quit over a row concerning his salary or because of a disagreement regarding management's decision to abandon a plan linking pay more closely with individual performance. The man had earned $30 million the previous year, although the bank lost money. Several of his traders had also defected despite the company's offer to increase bonuses to $45 million. Management considered the plan a compromise able to satisfy the individual trader's greed and at the same time a measure to protect the company's total earnings.[2]

Having made the grade, the trader usually pursues his profession until he runs out of steam. He may then move to other sectors of the bank or the securities house, reach his plateau or climb up the ladder. Some have risen to become president or chairman. Those who do not make the grade simply wind up on the legendary scrap heap for burnt-out traders.

CENTRAL BANKS AS SITTING DUCKS

In the early 1950s, long before the currency markets became the major battlefield between the international banking community and the European central banks, Milton Friedman, prophetically anticipating the coming of flexible exchange rates, forewarned:

> To suppose that speculation by governments would generally be profitable is in most cases equivalent to supposing that government officials risking funds that they do not themselves own are better judges of the likely movements in the foreign-exchange markets than private individuals risking their own funds.[3]

Indeed, for several years, gambling against the European central banks was a fabulous game providing fun and profits for the international banking community. Speculators borrowed currencies in the interbank market and sold them massively to the central banks, compelled by international agreement to absorb any quantity of their own currency in order to defend its parity. These bets were practically one-way, involving little risk; European central banks trying to keep their currencies within the bands of the exchange rate mechanism were easy targets for concerted attacks.

The mental contest between the guardians of the public treasure and the professional gamblers invariably ended in the same manner: central banks trying to arrest the onslaught with limited and precious reserves were outflanked, outwitted and finally crushed in chaotic confrontation by the overpowering might of limitless 'stateless' liquidity available in the interbank market.

With each crisis the capacity of the international financial community to undermine national monetary policies grew exponentially. As one banker put it, he attempted to get 'under the skin of the financial bureaucrats' to decide when it would pay to strike.

The ethos of the market is glorified by the theories of the economic Right which controls the financial press. Currency speculation is intellectually and morally justified by the market's self-proclaimed responsibility to signal governments that they are on the wrong economic course and that their currencies will be subject to pressures unless they correct their policies. Occasionally, academic luminaries will invest these theories with a halo.

From 1973 to 1979 the combined losses of the central banks of France, Germany, Italy, Japan, Switzerland, the United Kingdom and the United States exceeded $10 billion, making foreign-exchange intervention a costly government enterprise. During the crisis of September 1992 the Bank of England lost several billion pounds and again in July 1993 the central banks' defence strategy to maintain the ERM prompted the Bundesbank to throw DM60 billion on the market, in vain. Bundesbank president Helmut Schlesinger called it 'a high price to pay' for the support of weaker EC currencies.[4]

In this game, which lasted from the early 1970s to July 1993, the central banks consistently lost. The market struck before the impulses that make it move were understood by government experts. Central bank losses became a subsidy to private speculators and traders who gambled against their own or foreign governments.

Now the government-fed bonanza is over, but the banking community has won a resounding victory: all major currencies are floating and the market reigns supreme. The rules of the game have changed and the players gamble among themselves in a no man's land where everyone is by himself and everyone else's rival.

Floating rates mean volatility, real or potential, forcing commerce and industry to pay a premium for hedging. They also mean increased transaction charges. Each currency transaction necessarily involves a buyer and a seller, one heads up, the other tails down. The dealer may put the bank's money at risk or he may act at the request of a bank's client. Most of the market turnover is interbank dealing.

TO HEDGE OR NOT TO HEDGE?

That is the question facing people involved in international trade. Whether it is advisable to play it safe and pay a premium or carry the risk. The company treasurer may weigh the risks of not hedging against the cost of hedging, and still make the wrong decision. Unpredictable events overwhelming the market will upset his expectations. At the next quarterly board meeting he may have to admit an exchange loss and face an embarrassing explanation and uninformed criticism by people in top management who don't understand the workings of the market. He knows the insurance premium is substantial but it becomes part of the cost of doing business. He pays a levy for the privilege of sleeping well at night and for the security of having someone hold his hand. Banks try hard to persuade their clients to let them manage their currency exposure creatively in order to maximize gain and minimize risk.

The practitioners of the marketplace fall into several categories, depending on the forecasting techniques they use: momentum analysts, chartists, econometrists and so on. Self-appointed Nostradamuses profit from the fact that currency markets are shrouded in mystery, to offer their services. Several financial publications conduct yearly surveys of currency forecasters' track records and performance. The general conclusion is that forecasting expertise is a myth and that the gurus are 'hardly better than the toss of a coin'. The mystical world of foreign exchange forecasting only impresses those who are unfamiliar with it.

Derivatives, options and futures are not the panacea some people make them out to be. Many trusting treasurers with an appetite for risk but with little understanding of the sophisticated risk-management techniques, have found out that the cardinal principle of the financial markets is still *caveat emptor* – buyer beware.

In 1994 several customers of Bankers Trust – all large corporations – after having lost huge amounts of money in derivatives dealings, claiming they had been duped, sued the bank demanding compensation for losses and damages.[5]

IS DOOMSDAY COMING?

As risk control and risk management are top of the agenda in the foreign-exchange market, risk has become the shadowy passenger of global banking. Risk and reward travel side by side. As coded message transactions flash from dealing room to dealing room, each carries with it a possible gain and a downside potential. International banking, a rich man's game, has become a super-competitive profession, high-reward, high-risk and high-pressure, a tightrope exercise becoming occasionally a high-wire act.

Bull markets produce financial wizards; they disguise risk but do not eliminate it. Having made a lot of money, some people think they are particularly smart and can do just about anything. Then power goes to their heads and they tend to become reckless. Some banks or individuals might be tempted to take greater risks to keep up their profit stream. It would take only one major failure to trigger collateral calls and emergency close-outs throughout the foreign-exchange and derivatives market. Successful speculation is called enterprise, flunked speculation is considered blameable.

The precarious foundations upon which the structure rests, precarious in the face of the continuously growing flow of speculative funds, with short cycles of boom and bust, where the announcement of fabulous profits alternates with whispers of mass panics and the bursting of speculative bubbles, inevitably leads to intermittent spasms.

Celebrated accidents such as Bankhaus Herstatt and Continental Illinois served for some time as warnings that risk-taking can be fatal. When they occurred, markets reacted quickly; but the banking community will never be immune from this type of risk. Sooner or later another major dislocation may occur and it will be difficult to predict how far the chain reaction will go and who will be hurt.

Recent calamities are proof that banks have not lost their propensity to produce disasters of assorted kinds. Examples abound.

The trouble is memories are short. When a crisis breaks, the most important of all instincts – self-preservation – overrides all other considerations: everyone for himself, rescuing what can be saved at the expense of everyone else; just as during the banking panics of old. Like a house of cards they stand together and fall together. Ultimately, the stability of the market depends on the judgment, prudence and self-discipline of those who participate in it. In an atmosphere of increasing pressure and heightened competition, the potential for the erosion of responsible behaviour and prudent standards is a permanent menace. The occasional high-wire acts by employees and recurrent frauds by top management must serve as a reminder.

Are the international bankers sufficiently skilled to maintain liquidity in a suddenly shrinking market? Can they avoid inflicting disasters upon themselves and others? How to protect the banks from errors or misappropriations committed by their employees?

In April 1987 Merrill Lynch reported the largest loss in securities dealing in history. The firm had underwritten some $1.7 billion of mortgage-backed securities. Its senior trader secretly bought $800 million more. Interest rates suddenly started rising and the prices tumbled. Merril lost $377 million. One of the most sophisticated securities houses was in serious trouble because one person had taken on a massive unauthorized position and no one in control was aware of the operation.[5]

Banks are obviously loath to elaborate on question marks hanging over their currency losses. In 1994 Chemical Bank was one of the few admitting a $70 million loss, blaming it on a trader having gone beyond his position-risk limit.[6]

This, and all the other calamities that befell less prominent houses during the last decades, is a trifle compared with the series of disasters that struck the paragon of banking: Citicorp. As chairman of Citicorp, Walter Wriston had opened up unsuspected new frontiers and reached the pinnacle of the profession, admired and envied. First in everything, everywhere, he was the unrivalled matchless leader of the international banking profession. In the process he bore prime responsibility for the LDC (less developed countries) debt crisis which would last a decade and be partly resolved by the people he looked down on: the international financial organizations. After Wriston's retirement a new light was shed on his chairmanship. It was considered an 'anarchic, competitive culture, with its hunger for revenue rather than profit'.

> In August [1992] the bank revealed that the Federal Reserve Bank of New York and the Office of the Comptroller of the Currency (OCC) had required it to sign a memorandum of understanding (MoU) with them in February. This confirmed what was generally known that the regulators were – if not exactly camped outside the boardroom – keeping a close eye on the nation's largest bank. Outsiders asked what else, of perhaps greater and more sinister substance, the bank might be hiding.[7]

Unlike Continental Illinois, Citicorp did not go under, but its shareholders had to watch with dismay the descent from Wriston's adventurous forays. In 1990 alone they saw $5 billion of the market value of their shares evaporate.[8] We have come full circle: money is important only for what it will procure: goods and services. The frantic hustle-bustle of the trillion-dollar-a-day financial market leaves the rest of the universe mostly unawares. A global Las Vegas, it is a self-contained apprentice-wizard world, teeming with self-appointed gurus, with a crowd cheering loudly each new tradable product conjured up by one of its super-brains; a world where what is in today is out tomorrow and who is big today may be bust tomorrow. Largely divorced from industry and commerce, the conveyor-belt effect of a possible breakdown is difficult to ascertain or foresee. The stock market debacle of 1987 hardly produced a ripple in the real economy.

Every century has seen major speculative orgies, all ending with the inevitable crash: the most celebrated are the tulip bulb mania, the South Sea Bubble, John Law's Compagnie d'Occident, the crash of 1929. From time to time the market is gripped by irrational emotions, when it seems the sky is the limit. Then zest and rapture intoxicate the most cautious players, until suddenly the music stops, the gambling instinct demands its appropriate toll and the market destroys itself through overextension. The dream then becomes a nightmare.

At any time, once more, an unforeseeable insignificant occurrence somewhere, may spark a 'butterfly effect' spawning waves of deterministic chaos, wiping out paper fortunes and destroying lives, until the financial seism runs out of steam and the market settles upon its own debris on a new equilibrium that will stand the test of time, until the next crisis.

14 A Sisyphean Labyrinth

Since August 1993 the European Union has been passing through limbo like the European Monetary System it is supposed to administer. The demise of the ERM provoked frustration and bitterness on the Continent and jubilation in the international financial community. A few days after the breakup of the exchange rate mechanism *The Financial Times* published a postmortem analysis signed by seven MIT professors, including Nobel prize winner Paul Samuelson, expressing great satisfaction over the fact that Europe had finally abandoned the fixed-rate system. 'No reason to mourn,' the title claimed; 'Currency liberation could be good news for Europe's unemployed.'[1]

The essence of money power is now in the hands of the international financial community, while only the trappings are left with the political authorities. The claim that the freedom of capital movements brings great benefits in terms of the international allocation of investment is true in the sense that it provides a vehicle for corporations and individuals worldwide to invest easily in creditworthy borrowers while avoiding withholding taxes on their Eurobond interests. Free capital movements, however, have destroyed for years the dream of fixed parities, thus seriously impairing European commerce and industry, the main dupes of this state of affairs. Europe's industrial leadership has been perplexed, impotent and singularly mum.

Mr Akio Morita, founder and long-time chairman of Sony Corporation, undoubtedly spoke for the overwhelming majority of industrialists when he said that monetarists are 'handicapped by not knowing anything firsthand about industry'. He bemoaned the repercussions of floating currencies:

I believe the main problem is with our money. . . . For industrialists money is a scale. . . . Money speculators used one criterion only for buying one currency and selling another – profit. This resulted in a constant changing of rates that had nothing to do with industrial competitiveness. . . . This saps the will to work, to innovate, and a fundamental incentive in a free economic system is being lost. It is difficult to do business and make plans for the future without knowing what the value of your money will be. . . . This is why I continue to talk about the need for a new exchange-rate system based on industrial values rather than money markets. . . . Nations must get together to create a new international mechanism to stabilize rates. And the pursuit of monetary profits through mere speculation rather than productive endeavor must be discouraged.[2]

The bureaucratic system of checks and balances and its administrative complexities prevented the official decision-makers from understanding and interpreting relevant information, making reaction to market assaults ineffective. Policy-makers are subject to the normal human limitations of observing little and comprehending less. In the battle of wits between the governments establishing rules and private individuals moved by self-interest, trying by subtle and devious means to circumvent these rules, the advantage is easily on the side of those who dispose of worldwide financial market power. The controllers suffer from a standing handicap: they must begin by identifying and measuring the activities of the controlled; any chain of control is no stronger than its weakest link.

Inventive financial institutions, hiding behind a façade of polite proprieties, while constantly pioneering novel tricks in a permanently fluid environment, are too ingenious to be constrained by a simple set of non-discretionary rules. To be effective, the inventiveness of the guardians must match, and preferably surpass, the fertile resourcefulness of the poachers; this can hardly be expected. Official institutions have a marked tendency to accumulate layers of inertia and inefficiency in the financial as well as the economic and political domain; they are ill-equipped to cope with unanticipated problems.

The only official credibility the markets would recognize is one strong enough to deter speculative attacks by a threat of financial penalties. None of the capital controls, non-interest-bearing deposit schemes, capital charges or any other devices put temporarily into effect by various governments in the last few years to put sand in the wheels of capital movements, had any effect. Within a few days, market operators found loopholes.

In a world of floating rates, speculators can no more take easy money out of the central banks by pushing currencies to their limits. But the speculative funds presently latent in the market can be mobilized quickly and activated as soon as conditions for a possible crisis are in view. Speculators can wait quietly in ambush until propitious circumstances suddenly make them erupt into the open. They follow the planners like a shadow, ready to pour an avalanche of liquid funds on any attempt to reestablish a planified order in the currency markets. Bureaucratic policing and procedures constitute a maze enabling avoidance and evasion on the part of quick-witted recalcitrants refusing to submit to restrictions and regulations which they reject as a hindrance to free trade. In a contest between large administrative machines burdened with problems of gravity, comprehension, coordination, legal and administrative complexities, and the irrepressible ingenuity and chaotic but compact swiftness with which sophisticated private corporations wilfully circumvent official controls, the odds are against the guardians of the 'common good'.

THE NEXT ROUND

Since the crisis of July–August 1993 the markets have been relatively calm, ruffled only by occasional turbulences. The only difference is that now the financial operators decide; this does not prevent the finance ministers from congratulating themselves about their victory over the speculators. The international banking community has discovered its power to crack the system in a manner it is unlikely to forget. Governments are again discussing the next stages in the Maastricht process, almost as though nothing had happened. If they try to rebuild the system using the old drawings, their efforts will result in no more than another pious statement of objectives. The writing is already on the wall: they are bound to fall into the same old trap.

Between the 'believers' who have not learned the lesson and are convinced that political will, aided by a return to economic growth will, by itself, resurrect the system, still confident that the basic structures remain intact and can be reconditioned; the 'doubtful' who consider the timetable unrealistic, the 'pragmatists' who feel that the mechanism will have to be substantially reworked, the 'gradualists' recommending that the euro start operating in parallel to the national currencies, elaborate plans are once again under discussion.

We have experts on monetary affairs in Europe, bridging the worlds of banking and politics, theoreticians and practitioners. Confused by their contradictions and their uncertainty about the shape the Union should take, they lack a clear common vision of the priorities and the assurance of an agreed-upon goal.

Whether their grand conceptual schemes can, on D-day, contain the formidable reservoir of money power in the hands of the speculators, remains to be seen. The actors and the stakes are the same, the power game remains unchanged. The scenario is being written and the stage is set for the next round. There is no indication that the balance of power has shifted: the market is in command.

OF ALLOCATIONS AND PRIORITIES

The disruption of the currency markets has destabilized the European economy. Maintaining the sustained and balanced growth of the 1950s and 1960s would have been within easier reach and less unwieldy than the task of regenerating an out-of-gear society. The presence of 18 million unemployed overshadows the visible evidence that the overwhelming majority of people is still as well off and secure as before, and becoming more prosperous year after year. The peril is that the decline may have become irreversible, stabilizing itself or victimizing an ever increasing number.

If Europe is to rise to the challenge of sloping out of the recession in which its astounding post-war prosperity and a Capuan longing for a 'post-industrial society' – an economic eldorado – let it slide, it will have to table a different set of allocations and priorities. Over the past two decades millions of people have been mechanized out of their jobs because machines did the job better and more cheaply. Shifting masses of workers from industries where they have become permanently redundant and settling them in new workplaces has proved an impossible task. The problem is as much sociological and political as it is economic. It has induced a mental standstill. If the European economy is to be turned around, instead of sterile official incantation and an obsession with employment, the emphasis will have to shift to 'work' and the focus on innovation and entrepreneurial zeal. Keynesian pump priming has outlived its use.

Industry and commerce are among the few segments of society functioning satisfactorily. Goaded and constantly needled by competition, each unit has to be efficient or disappear. Value-adding industries, especially high-tech and engineering-intensive production units constitute the indispensable foundation of any industrialized economy. Only by adding value to raw materials through the application of high levels of knowledge and technology can the European economy compete again with the rest of the world. Europe is impaled on a dilemma: adjust its life-style to its productive capacity or adjust its productive capacity to its life-style? This implies the reintegration of the European economy into the globalized market. Japanese workloads and devotion – 'Asian values' – would be unenforceable; American financial and tax prestidigitation are out of reach. 'We're not ants,' the former French Prime Minister Edith Cresson said. 'We have the highest wages in Europe and I am proud of it,' a leader of the Belgian socialist trade union declared on television.

The pressure groups through which demands and grievances are filtered, prisoners of habit and ideologies, will have to give up some sacrosanct taboos and revise their self-evident beliefs. Straitjacketed by their sloganeering folklore around the social conquests of the past century, immersed in local class struggles, chasing enterprise away, they lack global vision; the more obtuse bear considerable responsibility for the industrial decline in several European countries. They expect the security of the centrally-planned economy and the financial advantages of the free-market system. Driven by the bovine power of custom they are unable to see the problem through.

Well-meaning legislation leading to overregulated labour markets and minimum wages, intended to protect the lower-paid, in fact destroys jobs massively and cripples the economy. Every succour produces its own perverse effects. Political solutions compelled by failure and crisis are easily invalidated by more failures and crises. If the European economy is to stagger out of its self-inflicted recession, this kind of mentality must be eradicated. The uninterrupted raising of labour's share has automatically reduced demand for labour; rationality on this subject, however, is banned from public discourse. The analysis is too severe.

Instead of sharing the fruits of a sluggish economy with a growing number of inactive people, the emphasis will have to shift to revitalization. More than 40 per cent of the 18 million unemployed in the European Union have been out of work for at least a year; five million have never worked at all.

Not everybody is unhappy with this dependency-creating system; many unemployed have come to consider the palliative as the norm:

> When four Dutch sociologists interviewed hundreds of people in three Dutch cities, they found that about 55 per cent of the long-term unemployed had stopped looking for work. More than half of this group had quit because they had found other activities to give meaning to their lives: hobbies, voluntary work, studying or working in the informal economy.[3]

A similar state of affairs, although officially ignored, presumably exists in every country. Security from the cradle to the grave – the expectation of a safe and predictable life – has blunted the creative spirit, which involves risk-taking.

It is no coincidence that the market economy has outlived the planned economy. Feasible alternatives to current policies should be probed. A different approach would be to create new jobs rather than keep people forever comfortable while getting by without working. This can only come about by dint of creativity by the vital few who are able to conceive and produce for the world markets attractive and innovative, engineering-intensive goods, appealing in function and design, thus creating demand and full-time industrial jobs. It is the only way for Europe to regain the position it once held. It will require a far-sighted strategy and a shift from the security of the welfare ethos – a European invention – to a renaissance of the entrepreneurial spirit, involving the task of rebuilding an industrial infrastructure, of adapting the educational system and of training motivated workers in the skills that are in demand. For too long education has been infused with an anti-utilitarian and anti-commercial bias. In Switzerland, Germany, Japan and Austria, countries with apprenticeship systems and vocational training, youth unemployment is hardly a problem, whereas in Italy and Spain it exceeds 30 per cent.

Successful economies have stayed ahead by moving incessantly to a higher level, which requires constantly better-educated workers. Work-training for the development of 'human capital', of marketable skills geared to the needs of tomorrow's economy is essential for the maintenance of a highly skilled, trained and performing workforce, indispensable in a competitive and expanding world economy. Sooner or later Europe will have to confront fundamental problems that are currently being evaded. If we are unable to change mentalities and restructure the economy, we will have to satisfy ourselves with what we have: permanent unemployment which, on the other hand, possibly constitutes, under present conditions, the only rampart against a built-in inflationary propensity. The cure might be worse than the disease.

In a world of constantly advancing technology, the power house and the nerve centre of any economy must be a front-line industry providing stable work opportunities in quantity and quality, from the drawing board to the laboratory, from the production line to the head office, logistics and support to sales and service. Financial, service organizations and bureaucracies have a role to play, mainly as support to value-adding industry. Finance should make venture capital available to nascent enterprise as well as to research and development for the future creation of new products. Europe is not ready for a 'junk bond' market which raises billions of dollars each year in the United States, where young firms have in the recent past imagined and created whole new industries: overnight-delivery business, software, wireless telephony and so on. Most of America's new jobs and an increasing proportion of its exports come from small firms.[4]

Venture capital has been sorely missing in Europe. Silicon Valley is unthinkable without it. Another contrast: in the United States, private capital is made available for potential profit. In Europe, too often, public funds have been distributed and dissipated in vain for political and social purposes, to dying or uncompetitive industries, dispensing the beneficiaries from making efforts to improve efficiency and profitability. The service sector can only survive if it has a productive manufacturing sector and a prosperous consumer society to serve.

In the field of industry and commerce the EU dream has turned somewhat sour. Europe's concentration on low-growth, low- and medium-tech industries has not been altered by the development of the common market. The opposite may be true. Between 1973 and 1985 the world market share of European exports of manufactured goods outside the EC fell by nearly 20 per cent, while intra-European trade in the same goods increased. Because the bulk of European trade was conducted within the EC, international competitiveness seemed satisfactory. But each country's export figures masked the fact that the total European export performance over that 12-year period was pathetic. Europeans have succumbed to the comforts and delights of overpaying themselves, buying from each other uncompetitively priced goods, unwanted elsewhere. Between 1986 and 1991 EC exports to world markets grew by 0.6 per cent a year while imports rose by 7 per cent. In five years the EC lost 4 per cent of world market share. And instead of improving, the situation worsens: in 1993 the European Union lost 9 per cent of its export volume against 1992. In job-creating high-tech and high-growth sectors the results are even worse. Misallocation of resources and priorities, and an obsession with *dirigiste* equalizing subsidies destined to create a 'convergence' of living standards among its members – inevitably the source of lobbying, fraud, mismanagement and corruption – are only among the most visible causes of this economic mediocrity. Venture capital is unavailable to young entrepreneurs, but large foreign corporations have unrestricted access to unlimited international financial resources.

European homes and offices are filled with sophisticated equipment bearing prestigious European names but manufactured outside Europe. Computers and software developed in the United States and produced in Far Eastern countries have become indispenable to the European economy. Television and hifi sets produced in Asia diffuse American entertainment; the children play with toys made in China.

While the competitive challenge of the global economy intensifies, while an automobile company such as BMW – to give just one example – delocalizes part of its production to establish a plant in the United States, the only solution combative trade unionists can think of is to reduce working hours. Instead of forcing manufacturers to delocalize, they should be encouraged to relocate in Europe. Before this happens, however, things may have to deteriorate much more. In 1994 BMW opened a $400 million factory in the United States in an area where workers earn barely half what BMW employees cost in Germany and where production costs are expected to be 30 per cent less. From there, cars will be exported to more than 100 countries. A Mercedes-Benz factory is due to open in Alabama by 1997.[5]

After World War II American wages stayed for many years the highest in the world, to the point that American industry priced itself out of the international markets. Between 1985 and 1993 American unit-labour costs in manufacturing declined by an average of 6.4 per cent a year compared with a rise of 6.6 per cent in Japan and 4.2 per cent in Germany.[6]

During the 1950s and 1960s American banking and industry invested in Europe, overriding the opposition of powerless unions. Today these investments pay off. The large international banks make the overwhelming bulk of their profits outside America, while a considerable number of companies, helped by creative accountants, derive a substantial part of their revenues from Europe and repatriate the profits. Europe has not and will not have anything of the like to fall back on.

While the European economies face an unstoppable decline, their dole queues stubbornly long, American factories are cranking at maximum capacity. During the 1980s many more jobs were created in the United States than in Europe; in private services they were three times as many as in France or Western Germany. Contrary to popular beliefs, the overwhelming majority of these jobs is in the managerial, professional, technical and administrative category. In Europe, because of government interference in the labour market, the capital market and the product market, the expansion of jobs in new industries and products is strangled. Well-intentioned and generous social benefits dissuade people from working out their own salvation; minimum-wage laws prevent the creation of unskilled jobs at the lower end of the pay spectrum.[7]

Instead of growth and prosperity, Europe faces declining competitiveness and convergence round depressed economies; a situation of its own making. Caught in the vicious circle of growing public deficits caused by increased unemployment, it confronts economic problems for which past experience provides no answer. Because of high labour costs, if and when recovery comes, it is likely to be productivity-driven rather than job-driven. The interplay of politics and economics generally leads to a situation where the political purpose takes precedence over economic apprehension, where political judgment is applied to economic problems; good politics can make bad policy. Unless policies and priorities are adjusted to the requirements of a dynamic global economy, the end of the twentieth century may witness a period when the European-style 'mixed-economy' system goes awry because the men who have taken upon themselves its management did not quite understand its workings.

CONVERGENCE IS NOT ENOUGH

Could a common currency be the panacea, the *deus ex machina* ready-made to solve Europe's shortcomings? Can the euro cure or even alleviate Europe's sclerotic afflictions, namely excessively high government budget deficits and globally uncompetitive industries?

Since the monetary upheavals of 1992 and 1993 relative calm has returned to the dealing rooms; inflation is receding everywhere. Lulled by this unwonted truce after years of turmoil, official circles parade the fiction that their policies, after all, were right; they seem to believe their own rhetoric. They overlook the fact that the international banking community – the speculators – has absolute control over the market; obviously also, the latent inflationary pressures are currently contained, not by fiscal or monetary policies, but by overriding popular expectations of a worsening recession. Undoubtedly, people in commerce and industry want stability above all, so they can plan their business and invest for the medium and long term as demand develops, and not be tossed around by the erratic swings of boom and bust. Professional market operators, however, thrive on floating rates and volatility, and they are in command, ready to torpedo or whipsaw any new system in the bud. And what is more: they have clearly warned over and over again: 'don't try'. They have behind them the combined might of the Anglo-Saxon political and financial community and undoubtedly of a large, if discreet, contingent of European bankers.

The plain fact is that getting back to narrow bands would mean once again confronting the foreign-exchange markets more than ever self-conscious of their powers.

The men who manage international monetary affairs are the central bankers and the finance ministers. In the United States, the Treasury is traditionally – with exceptions – in the hands of a closed circle, made up of the sharpest financial minds who shuttle between a banking career and government service. To them the business of government is a government of business. Enjoying for a couple of years the 'motorcade syndrome' and the prestige of being called 'Mr Secretary' for the rest of one's days more than compensates for a temporarily reduced salary.

In Europe, finance ministers are political 'generalists' selected for their supposed ability to hold the purse strings of domestic finances. There is an endemic belief, in politics, that an expert becomes such by appointment to the appropriate position. In Europe, ministers shuttle with equal competence between agriculture, defence or foreign affairs. Usually finance ministers are out of office and replaced before they really understand what it is all about and before they can do much good – or harm. They are advised by experts, civil servants, grown up in government office, working their way to senior posts through specialized knowledge and routine activities. Capable and informed as they may be, their imagination and initiatives are chained to their function as lieutenants.

Elected politicians, finance ministers share the responsibility for monetary policy with central bankers, appointed civil servants. In Europe, the Bundesbank, all by itself, has been the conscience, the vigil and the guardian of monetary stability, while in France, Italy and elsewhere governments resorted to the elixir of pump priming.

The recurrent confrontational relationship between European monetary authorities and the international banking community in the wake of the liberalization and globalization of the financial markets during the 1960s and 1970s, ended in a total debacle for the guardians of national currencies. Individually and collectively they were unable to stave off the attackers. Generally, instead of presenting a united front against the speculators, they were at variance with each other. It has been a hard lesson. They had inherited the rules of the game set by their predecessors at a time when life was simpler. The textbook prescriptions of the old guard are anachronistic and passé. To get back to narrow bands on a set timetable will mean once again confronting the foreign-exchange markets: a recipe for trouble.

If they want to regain control over what they consider their legitimate domain, the central bankers will have to display uncommon intellectual amperage: creative ingenuity, economic expertise, market savvy, political dexterity, solidarity and more. Elaborate systems conceived in self-righteousness are an inadequate match for the centralized but globally operating financial markets, where corporate interest and corporate power take precedence over the rule of foreign law. The European Monetary Institute has been established in Frankfurt, but London will remain for a long time the world centre of financial power. The promised land of monetary union is not in sight.

The logistics to get from here to there will be superlatively complex and costly. From the rejiggering of computer systems to the conversion of accounts by large corporations as well as small shopkeepers, either in a progressive process involving dual accounting or through a chaotic and unimaginable 'big bang', the complications are staggering. Is the game worth the candle?

If the monetary union is not to join the Werner Plan, the Snake and the EMS on the shelves of discards of EU archives, its promoters will have to arm themselves with more than economics; re-reading and meditating the precepts and advice of Machiavelli and Clausewitz may be useful but not sufficient. A sixth sense and a touch of Keynesian clairvoyance are prerequisites. Complacency will be a major pitfall. If a trillion-dollar-a-day foreign-exchange market does not scare or impress them, they face rude awakenings. After 25 years of Sisyphean labours and the resultant relics of three grandiose plans, the monetary union is a shambles. Impervious planners have again resolutely and confidently undertaken the long march up a three-stage blind alley, armed with deadlines and convergence criteria, allowing dogma to overshadow common sense.

Taking on the presidency of the European Commission in January 1995, Jacques Santer declared: 'The monetary turbulences of August 1993 have been overcome with greater ease than expected. Instead of collapsing, as had been feared, the European Monetary System has been strenghtened.'[8]

Stable currencies are one of the necessary ingredients of European recovery. The concept of a single currency was the product of visionary political imagination. Innovative and intuitively appealing, it has acquired over the years a sentimental and symbolic value. Whether it would be economically beneficial if instituted, is a moot question.

Notes

1 The Power of Money

1   J. K. Galbraith, *Money* (Boston: Houghton Mifflin, 1975), p. 5.
2   M. Friedman and A. Jacobson Schwartz, *A Monetary History of the United States, 1867–1960* (Princeton: Princeton University Press, 1963), p. 676.

2 The Morganization of America

1   L. Corey, *The House of Morgan* (New York: G. Howard Watt, 1930), p. 89.
2   R. Sobel, *Panic on Wall Street* (New York: Collier Books, 1968), p. 317.
3   L. Corey, *The House of Morgan*, p. 349.
4   Ibid., pp. 352–6.
5   Ibid., p. 446.
6   Ibid., p. 449.
7   R. J. Barnet and R. E. Müller, *Global Reach* (New York: Simon and Schuster, 1974), p. 235.
8   W. B. Wriston, *Risk & Other Four-Letter Words* (New York: Harper & Row, 1986), pp. 144 and 182.
9   M. Mayer, *The Money Bazaars* (New York: E. P. Dutton, 1984), p. 233.
10 P. Volcker and T. Gyohten, *Changing Fortunes* (New York: Times Books, 1992), pp. 216–21.

3 Germany Will Pay

1   G. Clemenceau, *Grandeurs et Misères d'une Victoire* (Paris: Plon, 1930), p. 152.
2   Ibid., p. 262.
3   J. M. Keynes, *The Economic Consequences of the Peace* (London: Macmillan, 4th ed. 1971), pp. 158–9.
4   W. Vocke, *Memoiren* (Stuttgart: Deutsche Verlags-Anstalt, 1973), p. 85.
5   H. Coston, *L'Europe des Banquiers* (Paris: Documents et Témoignages, 1963), pp. 192–5.
6   Address by the Right Hon. Viscount D'Abernon on 26 November 1926, quoted in *Euromoney*, July 1977, pp. 146–7.
7   K. Singer, *Staat und Wirtschaft seit dem Waffen stillstand* (Iena: Gustav Fischer, 1924), pp. 195–8.
8   S. A. Schuker, *The End of French Predominance in Europe* (Chapel Hill: University of North Carolina Press, 1967), p. 5.
9   M. Baumont, *La Faillite de la Paix, 1918–1939* (Paris: Presses Universitaires de France, 1945), p. 143.

10 C. Bresciani-Turroni, *The Economics of Inflation* (London: Allen & Unwin, 1937), pp. 100–2.
11 Ibid., pp. 105–6.
12 K. Heiden, *Der Fuehrer, Hitler's Rise to Power*, transl. R. Manheim (Boston: Houghton Mifflin, 1944), pp. 125–40.
13 H. Schacht, *76 Jahre meines Lebens* (Bad Wörishofen: Kindler und Schiermeyer Verlag, 1953), pp. 232–3.
14 H. Schacht, *The Magic of Money*, transl. P. Erskine (London: Oldbourne, 1967), p. 72.

4 Morgan's Solution

1 Fr. Leith-Ross, *Money Talks* (London: Hutchinson, 1968), p. 84.
2 J. M. Keynes, *A Revision of the Treaty*, 3rd ed. (London: Macmillan, 1971), p. 111.
3 H. Schacht, *The Magic of Money*, pp. 43–7.
4 *The Economist*, 19 Dec. 1925.
5 L. Corey, *The House of Morgan*, p. 432.
6 H. Schacht, *The Magic of Money*, p. 138.

5 The Crash

1 J. K. Galbraith, *Money*, p. 168.
2 D. E. Moggridge, *The Return to Gold*, 1925 (Cambridge: University Press, 1969)
3 J. K. Galbraith, *Money*, pp. 178–9.
4 P. A. Samuelson, *Economics*, 6th ed. (New York: McGraw-Hill, 1964), p. 698.
5 *The Economist*, 12 Sept. 1931.
6 D. E. Moggridge, *The Return to Gold* p. 9.
7 *The Economist*, 17 June 1961.
8 *The Economist*, 20 June 1931.
9 *The New Statesman and Nation*, 15 Aug. 1931.
10 *The Economist*, 1 Aug. 1931.

6 The Wasted Years

1 *The Economist*, 4 Feb. 1933.
2 *The Economist*, 17 Jan. 1931, p. 108.
3 J. M. Blum, *Roosevelt and Morgenthau* (Boston: Houghton Mifflin, 1972), pp. 45–6.
4 Ibid, pp.76-7.
5 Ibid p. 84.
6 *The Economist*, 2 Oct. 1937.
7 Ibid., 16 Oct. 1937.
8 Ibid., 28 Feb. 1942.
9 Ibid., 6 May 1939.
10 Ibid., 29 Jan. 1938.

11 Ibid., 2 Jan. 1937.
12 Ibid., 8 Aug. 1936.
13 Ibid., 5 Dec. 1936
14 Ibid., 5 Nov. 1938.
15 W. Vocke, *Memoiren*, pp. 103–10.

7 Bretton Woods Revisited

1 Morgenthau Diary 755, p. 71, Franklin D. Roosevelt Library, Hyde Park, NY.
2 Morgenthau Diary 756, pp. 46–52.
3 House Bretton Woods Hearings, 1:152 (15 March 1945).
4 Correspondence of the Foreign Office, 371/45664, Keynes letter to Brand, 5 April 1945, London: Public Record Office.
5 Correspondence of the Foreign Office, 371/45662, Keynes Memorandum. 29 December 1944.
6 Morgenthau Diary 749, pp. 224–37.
7 Goldenweiser Papers, Bretton Woods Conference, RG 59, Box 4, National Archives, Washington, DC.
8 *New York Herald Tribune*, 31 March 1946.
9 J. M. Blum, *Roosevelt and Morgenthau* p. 647.
10 Morgenthau Diary 639, p. 23.
11 *New York Herald Tribune*, 21 Nov. 1943.
12 *Commercial and Financial Chronicle*, 6 May 1943.
13 *Völkischer Beobachter*, 11 April 1943.
14 *Christian Science Monitor*, 27 Feb. 1945.
15 *Milwaukee Journal*, 14 Feb. 1945.
16 Morgenthau Diary 807, pp. 151–6.
17 *New York Times*, 5 Feb. 1945.
18 Morgenthau Diary 816, pp. 108–18.
19 Congressional Record, Senate, 16 July 1945, p. 7573.
20 Congressional Record, House, 5 June 1945, p. 5541.
21 Ibid., 6 June 1945, p. 5675.
22 Ibid., 5 June 1945, p. 5590.
23 Ibid., 6 June 1945, p. 5668.
24 Ibid., 6 June 1945, p. 5671.
25 Ibid., 19 July 1945, p. 7762.

8 The Americanization of Europe

1 E. A. McCreary, *The Americanization of Europe* (New York: Doubleday, 1964), p. 4.
2 *Forbes*, 1 Jan. 1972, p. 24.
3 *Euromoney*, Jan. 1970, pp. 4 and 6.
4 R. Solomon, *The International Monetary System, 1945–1976* (New York: Harper & Row, 1977), p. 36.
5 Ibid., p. 54.

6   J. Rueff, *Le Péché Monétaire de l'Occident* (Paris: Plon, 1971), pp. 24, 179 and 219.
7   Quoted in W. Slotosch: *Panorama der Weltinflation* (Munich: Kurt Desch, 1971), pp. 191–3.
8   R. Solomon, *The International Monetary System* p. 63.
9   K. W. Dam, *The Rules of the Game* (Chicago: University of Chicago Press, 1982), p. 248.
10 G. L. Weil and I. Davidson, *The Gold War* (London: Secker & Warburg, 1970), pp. 126–31.
11 *Der Spiegel*, No. 41, 1971, p. 32.
12 *Business Week*, 8 May 1971.
13 M. Moffitt, *The World's Money* (New York: Simon and Schuster, 1983), p. 39.
14 *New York Herald Tribune*, 20 Aug. 1971.
15 *Der Spiegel*, No. 41, 1971, p. 32.
16 Ibid., No. 20, 1971, p. 21.
17 *The Economist*, 28 Aug. 1971.
18 *The Wall Street Journal*, 4 Aug. 1971.
19 *The Economist*, 28 Aug. 1971.
20 Ibid., 28 Aug. 1971.
21 *International Herald Tribune*, 1 March 1972.
22 *International Herald Tribune*, 24 Sept. 1971.
23 *International Herald Tribune*, 19 Oct. 1971.
24 *New York Times*, 17 Oct. 1971.
25 P. A. Volcker and T. Gyohten, *Changing Fortunes* p. 85.
26 Ibid., pp. 85–6.
27 Quoted in *Euromoney*, Jan. 1972, p. 54.
28 *The Wall Street Journal*, 7 March 1972.
29 *International Herald Tribune*, 18 May 1972.
30 Ibid., 18 May 1972.
31 W. Slotosch, *Panorama der Weltinflation*, p. 190.

9 The Eurodollar

1   H.V. Prochnow and H.V. Prochnow Jr, *The Changing World of Banking* (New York: Harper & Row, 1974), p. 100.
2   P. Einzig, *Parallel Money Markets* (London: Macmillan, 1971), p. 144.
3   J. Montaldo, *Les Secrets de la Banque Soviétique en France* (Paris: Albin Michel, 1979).
4   J. Attali, *Un Homme d'Influence* (Paris: Fayard, 1985), pp. 328–30.
5   P. Einzig, *Foreign Dollar Loans in Europe* (London: Macmillan, 1965), pp. VI–VII.
6   P. E. Volcker and T. Gyothen, *Changing Fortunes*, p. 33.
7   W. R. Neikirk, *Volcker, Portrait of the Man* (New York: Congdon & Weed, 1987), p. 124.
8   *Euromoney*, Dec. 1970, p. 14.
9   J. Attali, *Un Homme d'Iufluence*, pp. 383–4.
10 *The Wall Street Journal*, Europe, Brussels, 15 Dec. 1994.

10 Europe Unite

1 J. J. Kaplan and G. Schleiminger, *The European Payments Union* (Oxford: Clarendon Press, 1989), p. 13.
2 Ibid., p. 19.
3 Ibid., p. 22.
4 Ibid., pp. 103–4.
5 L. Erhard, *Wohlstand für Alle* (Düsseldorf: Econ-Verlag, 1957), p. 18.
6 W. Vocke, *Memoiren,* pp. 192–3.
7 J. J. Kaplan and G. Schleiminger, *The European ayments Union* p. 152.
8 *Interlocking Subversion in Government Departments The Harry Dexter White Papers*: (Washington, DC: US Government Printing Office, 1955), part 30, pp. 2637–43.
9 *Der Spiegel*, 3 May 1971.
10 W. Vocke, *Memoiren* p. 164.
11 M. T. Sumner and G. Zis, *European Monetary Union* (London: Macmillan, 1982), p. 232.
12 P. Ludlow, *The Making of the European Monetary System* (London: Butterworth Scientific, 1982), p. 91.
13 Quoted in Ibid, pp. 106–7.
14 Ibid, p. 111.
15 Quoted in Ibid, pp. 112–13.
16 Ibid., p. 119.
17 Ibid, p. 138.
18 Ibid., p. 185.
19 Ibid., p. 197.
20 Ibid., p. 199.
21 Ibid., p. 249.

11 The EMU House of Cards

1 Reuter telex, 13 Sept. 1992.
2 *The Independent*, 17 Sept. 1992.
3 Reuter telex, 17 Sept. 1992.
4 *The Independent*, 17 Sept. 1992.
5 *International Herald Tribune*, 18 Sept. 1992.
6 *The Economist*, 19 Sept. 1992.
7 *The Times*, 22 Sept. 1992.
8 Reuter telex, 13 April 1993.
9 *Der Spiegel*, Nr. 15, 1993.
10 *The Financial Times*, 26 May 1993.
11 *The Wall Street Journal*, 23 June 1993.
12 *International Herald Tribune*, 13 July 1993.
13 *Le Monde*, 26 July 1993.
14 *The Financial Times*, 8 Oct. 1993.
15 *Euromoney,* Oct. 1977, p. 127.
16 Quoted in *The Financial Times*, 2 Aug. 1993.
17 Ibid.

18 Ibid.
19 *The Financial Times,* 3 Aug. 1993.
20 *Süddeutsche Zeitung,* 3 Aug. 1993.
21 *The Times,* 5 Aug. 1993.
22 Ibid.
23 *Süddeutsche Zeitung,* 3 Aug. 1993.
24 *The Wall Street Journal,* Europe, Brussels, 5 Aug. 1993.
25 Ibid., 3 Aug. 1993.
26 *Die Welt,* 3 Aug. 1993.
27 *The Financial Times,* 7 Aug. 1993.
28 *Der Spiegel,* 9 Aug. 1993.
29 *The Times,* 3 Aug. 1993
30 Reuter telex, 12 Aug. 1993.
31 *The Economist,* 25 Dec. 1993.

12 Banking in Wonderland

1 J.W. Beyen, *Money in a Maelstrom* (New York: Macmillan, 1949), p. 53.
2 P. Samuelson, *Economics* p. 151.
3 H. Schacht, *The Magic of Money* p. 76.
4 W. B. Wriston, *Risk & Other Four-Letter Words* pp. 25, 31 and 182.
5 Ibid., p. 146.
6 *Euromoney,* June 1979, p. 7.
7 Ibid., Oct. 1983, p. 299.
8 P. A. Volcker and T. Gyothen, p. 316.
9 *Euromoney,* April 1979, p. 13.
10 Ibid., p. 11.
11 P. A. Volcker and T. Gyothen, *Changing Fortunes,* pp. 215–16.
12 M. Moffitt, *The World's Money,* pp. 149–157.

13 The Global Money Game

1 *Euromoney,* Nov. 1987, p. 87.
2 *The Economist,* 1 July 1995, pp. 77–9.
3 Quoted in *Euromoney,* Nov. 1980, p. 123.
4 Reuter telex, 2 Aug. 1993.
5 *The Economist,* 19 Nov. 1994, pp. 87–8.
6 *Euromoney,* May 1991, p. 31.
7 *The Economist,* 7 Jan. 1995.
8 *Euromoney,* Dec. 1992, p. 31.

14 A Sisyphean Labyrinth

1 *The Financial Times,* 6 Aug. 1993.
2 Akio Morita and Sony, *Made in Japan* (London: HarperCollins, 1994), pp. 294–300.
3 *The Economist,* 30 July 1994, p. 19.
4 Ibid., 15 Jan. 1994, p. 66.

5   Ibid., 19 Nov. 1994, p. 77.
6   Ibid., 15 Jan. 1994, p. 66.
7   *The OECD Jobs Study, Evidence and Explanations*, Paris 1994.
8   *Le Soir*

Index